MW01234242

GREAT
ESCAPES

Escapes from Nazi Persecution

Stephen Currie

LUCENT
BOOKS®

THOMSON
GALE

San Diego • Detroit • New York • San Francisco • Cleveland • New Haven, Conn. • Waterville, Maine • London • Munich

LIBRARY OF CONGRESS CATALOGING-IN-PUBLICATION DATA

Currie, Stephen, 1960–
    Escapes from Nazi persecution / by Stephen Currie.
        v. cm. — (Great escapes)
Includes bibliographical references and index.
Contents: Hitler and the Nazis—East from Lithuania—Escape from Auschwitz—Escape from Colditz—Out of Denmark—Attack at Sobibor.
    ISBN 1-59018-279-0 (hard. alk. paper)
1. World War, 1939–1945—Prisoners and prisons, German. 2. Escapes. 3. Holocaust, Jewish (1939–1945) 4. Concentration camps—Europe. 5. Prisoners of war—Germany—History—20th century. [1. World War, 1939–1945—Prisoners and prisons, German. 2. Holocaust, Jewish (1939–1945) 3. Auschwitz (Concentration camp) 4. Sobibor (Concentration camp) 5. Concentration camp escapes.] I. Title. II. Series.
D805.A2C87 2004
940.53'185—dc21
                                      2003005443

Contents

Foreword

THE NOTION OF escape strikes a chord in most of us. We are intrigued by tales of narrow deliverance from adversity and delight in the stories of those who have successfully skirted disaster. When a few seemingly chosen people are liberated from a fate that befalls many others, we feel that to some degree the larger injustice has been rectified; that in their freedom, a small bit of justice prevailed.

Persecution and disaster, whether in nature or from what has frequently been called "man's inhumanity to man," have been all too common throughout history. Fires, floods, and earthquakes have killed millions; enslavement, inquisitions, and so-called ethnic cleansing millions more. Time and again, people have faced what seems to be certain death and looked for a way out. The stories of these escapes reveal the emotional and physical strength of our fellow human beings. They are at once dramatic, compelling, and inspirational.

Some of these escapes have been entirely the work of one brave person. Others have involved hundreds or even thousands of people. Escapees themselves vary; some seek to return to a life they have lost, others flee to a life they have only dreamed of, still others are simply fugitives against time. Their stories enlighten even the darkest events of history, making it clear that wherever there is determination, courage, and creativity, there is hope. Dr. Viktor E. Frankl, a survivor of four Nazi concentration camps, expressed this tenacity in the following way: "Everything can be taken from a man but one thing: the last of human freedoms—to choose one's attitude in any given set of circumstances—to choose one's own way."

People who are mired in captivity become willing to chance the unknown at any cost. Americans who escaped from slavery, for example, escaped toward a vision that the life they had never been allowed to live would offer them new hope. Fugitive slaves had no inkling of what life in free territory would hold for them, or if they would even make it there alive. Fears of the unknown, however, were outweighed by the mere possibility of living a free life.

While many escapes involve careful and intricate planning, no path of flight follows a fixed blueprint. Most escapes owe their success to on-the-spot improvisation and keen resourcefulness. A piece of clothing found at a critical juncture might be just the thing out of which to fashion a cunning disguise; a brick lying harmlessly in the corner of a room might provide just enough support to boost a person through the crack in a window.

Conversely, fate may carelessly toss many pitfalls at the feet of those in flight. An unexpected flood might render a road impassable; a sympathetic train conductor might be suddenly fired, replaced with an unfriendly stranger. All escapes are both hindered and helped by such blind chance. Those fleeing for their lives must be nimble enough to dodge obstacles and snatch at opportunities that might affect their chances along the way.

It is common for people who have undergone such ordeals to question whether their salvation came to them by chance, or if they were somehow chosen for a greater scheme, a larger purpose. All become changed people, bestowed with a grand sense of purpose and a rich appreciation for life. It is this appreciation for life too that draws us to their stories, as they impress upon us the importance of living every day to its fullest, and inspire us to find ways to escape from our own prisons.

Lucent's Great Escapes series describes some of the most remarkable escapes in history. Each volume chronicles five individual stories on a common topic. The narratives focus on planning, executing, and surviving the escapes. The books quote liberally from primary sources, while ample background information lends historical context. An appendix of primary sources is also included in each volume, sharing additional stories of escape not profiled in the main text. Endnotes, two bibliographies, maps of escape routes, and sidebars enhance each volume.

Introduction

Hitler and the Nazis

IN THE LATE 1920s, a small political party known as the National Socialists began to attract attention in Germany. The National Socialists, or Nazis as they soon were called, were led by an Austrian-born politician named Adolf Hitler. They advocated a political philosophy known as fascism. A fascist government consolidates power in one strong leader with the military at his disposal; it puts little focus on individual rights and freedoms. Wildly patriotic, often menacing, and eager to change the way the country was run, Hitler and the Nazis steadily gained popular support over the next few years.

By 1933, the Nazis had become a major presence in German politics. In January, Hitler was asked to take the position of chancellor in a coalition government—that is, a government jointly run by more than one party. Although the Nazis were opposed by most Germans, this was the opportunity Hitler had been waiting for. Through intimidation, lies, and a clever use of the German constitution, he swiftly took over the government. At the end of March, Germany was firmly in Hitler's hands.

Hitler and the Nazis would remain in control of Germany until the end of World War II in 1945. During the Hitler years, the Nazi Party ruled Germany with violence and brutality. Free speech was not permitted; neither was political dissension. Germany became a police state, with thousands of officers patrolling the streets of German cities and towns and a network of informers spying on their neighbors. As for dissidents, they were exiled, imprisoned, or killed.

Persecution

Although the Nazis had policies and opinions about economics, forms of government, and other matters, their philosophy was in large part constructed upon racism. The Nazis subscribed to a racial theory that valued certain ethnic groups more than others. At the top of this list were the so-called Aryans—northern Europeans in general, and Germans in particular. These people, Hitler believed, were genetically pure and strong. In his words, they were "the highest species of humanity on earth."[1]

At the bottom of Hitler's list, on the other hand, were the Jews. The Jewish people had lived in Europe for more than two thousand years. Through most of that time their Christian neighbors had treated them with scorn and suspicion; anti-Semitism—or anti-Jewish feeling—was prevalent. Nevertheless, Jews had usually been tolerated by the Christian majority, and despite the oppression, Judaism often thrived. In some cities of eastern Europe, Jews made up as much as one-fourth of the population. And some of Europe's most prominent thinkers, business leaders, and artists had been Jews.

But Hitler hated the Jews with a passion. To him, Jews were not simply of inferior stock; in his eyes, their mere existence polluted and corrupted those

around them. Immediately after taking office, he declared a nationwide boycott of Jewish businesses. The boycott soon escalated to anti-Jewish laws, and then to violence and mass arrests of Germany's Jews. By 1938, Hitler had annexed nearby Austria, and the persecution spread there as well. Unwilling to live in an oppressive Nazi regime, thousands of Jews decided to leave Germany and Austria.

Hitler stands above the crowd and sternly salutes at a 1928 Nazi rally in Nuremberg.

Things soon grew worse for those in Europe who opposed the Nazis. Hitler was eager to control as much of Europe as he could. In 1939, his armies attacked Poland, thus beginning World War II. The countries that opposed the Nazis—the Allies, headed at first by Britain and France—proved poorly prepared to fight the German armies. As a result, the Germans overran one country after another: Czechoslovakia, Belgium, the Netherlands, and France itself. As Germany's armies spread across Europe, more and more people came under the thumb of the Nazis.

The Final Solution

With the passage of time, Nazism became ever more brutal. Early in his rule, Hitler's goal had not been so much to kill Jews and other "undesirables" as to make them leave for other countries.

Concentration Camps

Ravensbruck

Sachsenhausen

Treblinka

Chelmno

Sobibor

GERMAN-OCCUPIED POLAND

Belzec

GERMANY

Buchenwald

Auschwitz

PROTECTORATE OF BOHEMIA-MORAVIA

SLOVAKIA

Dachau

Large-Scale Labor Camps

Large-Scale Extermination Camps

Soon after the outbreak of war, though, that policy changed. Increasingly, Hitler and his fellow Nazis became convinced that it was time to apply a so-called Final Solution to what they termed Europe's "Jewish problem." In a 1942 speech, Hitler spelled out that solution: His goal, he announced, would be "the complete annihilation of the Jews."[2]

The Nazis carried out this task with brutality and a chilling efficiency. Herding Jews into neighborhoods called ghettos, Nazi guards sealed off access from the outside world and watched as the Jews inside starved to death. The German government built prisons called concentration camps, too, and shipped Jews to them from all across Europe. Most were death camps at which thousands of victims were put to death in the course of a single day—victims whose only crime was that their existence offended the Nazis. The murders continued almost until the last day of the war in Europe. Today, this slaughter is known as the Holocaust.

Although it is impossible to know the exact death toll of the Holocaust, it is clear that the loss of life was unimaginably high. About 6 million Jews alone perished in the Holocaust. Another 5 million non-Jews, or gentiles, are usually counted as victims of the Holocaust as well. This group includes political opponents, homosexuals, the handicapped, gypsies, and other groups deemed dangerous or unwanted by the Nazis; it also includes prisoners of war, especially from the Soviet Union. In

Émigrés

Among the well-known Jews who fled the Nazi-controlled territories of Europe were scientist Albert Einstein, psychoanalyst Sigmund Freud, and artist Marc Chagall. But Jews were not the only ones to leave. A number of gentiles, or non-Jews, who disagreed with Nazi policies did the same. The German writer Thomas Mann, for instance, left Germany soon after the Nazis came to power. So did Christian theologian Paul Tillich, playwright Bertolt Brecht, and the Von Trapp family of Austria, later featured in the film *The Sound of Music*. Fearing retribution, non-Jewish political leaders, trade unionists, and others who had spoken out against the Nazis often decided to flee as well.

all, the Holocaust resulted in the deaths of approximately 11 million people.

Escape

Under these conditions, escape from the Nazis was essential. Those targeted for oppression were in danger of losing their property, their freedom, their families, and their lives. Unfortunately, as the years wore on, escape became more and more difficult. Not only did Nazi brutality grow stronger, but escape opportunities became increasingly rare. It was harder to escape from a guarded Jewish ghetto than from a small country town. It was harder still to escape from a concentration camp.

But Jews and other oppressed peoples in Nazi Europe did manage to escape from the brutality and the persecution of their enemies. People escaped from small towns and from large cities, from prisons and ghettoes; even, in a few cases, from concentration camps themselves. Those who escaped had to use every resource at their disposal. Some disguised themselves and manufactured phony documents in order to smuggle themselves out of Nazi-occupied zones. Others hid for months or years in mountains, forests, and even urban sewers, waiting for an opportunity to make a break for freedom. Even those with legal permission to leave Nazi territory, relatively common early in Hitler's reign, were often risking their lives; there was no guarantee that guards and soldiers would respect their rights, and no guarantee that angry pro-Nazi crowds would leave them alone.

The stories of those who escaped from Nazi persecution are harrowing, but they provide a glimmer of hope. The actions of a brave and dedicated few demonstrate the human ability to resist and defy evil, even under the most wretched of circumstances. Every person who escaped from Nazi persecution served as a reminder of a basic truth: Evil, vicious, and brutal as the Nazis were, they were not all-powerful.

East from Lithuania

NOT EVERY ESCAPE from Nazi persecution actually took place in Nazi-controlled territory. By the late 1930s, it had become abundantly clear that Hitler intended to conquer as much of Europe as he could. Fearing that their homes would soon be overrun by Nazi troops, many Jews who lived in areas not yet controlled by Germany began to make plans to leave.

In theory, it should have been easy enough for these Jews to make their way somewhere else. Their emigration should have been a simple move from one country to another, not a dangerous and frightening escape. But because of political considerations and widespread prejudice, it proved almost impossible for many of Europe's Jews to find homes elsewhere. Despite their best efforts, many did not manage to make it to safety before the Nazis arrived. And those who did had to rely on good fortune and the good will of others to escape the onrushing Nazis—even when the Nazis were not yet in sight.

Lithuania

During the early stages of World War II, the eastern European nation of Lithuania became a favored destination for Jews fleeing Nazism. As Germany smashed the defenses of nearby countries, Jews from Austria, Czechoslovakia, and other areas of central and eastern Europe began to pour into Lithuanian territory in search of refuge. Jews from western Europe arrived, too. By early 1940, about 250,000 Jews lived in Lithuania. The population of native-born Jews had been supplemented by thousands more refugees

Lithuanian Jews move their belongings into a ghetto in 1941. Some Jews were fortunate enough to evade the ghetto and escape from Lithuania.

from nations as close as Poland and as distant as the Netherlands.

The refugees' journey to Lithuania was often extremely difficult. The risk of being captured or killed by Nazi soldiers was great, and the local populations were often nearly as brutal toward Jews. Hunger, disease, and weather also made travel hazardous. "The weather had grown bitterly cold," recalled one anonymous Polish traveler, "and many froze to death."[3] Others, however, did reach their destination. A few disguised themselves to hide their Jewish identity. Others slipped through the countryside; one man took two months to cover a distance that would have taken less than a day by train.

Still, the journey seemed worth it. In the early days of the war, Lithuania ap-

peared to be safe. A small country on the shores of the Baltic Sea, Lithuania had a justifiable reputation as a tolerant and cosmopolitan place. "The government," remembered Lithuanian-born Jew Zev Birger, "was truly liberal toward the Jewish minority."[4] Indeed, the city of Vilnius, or Vilna, was one of the most important centers of Jewish culture anywhere in the world. Its contributions to Judaism had earned it the nickname the "Jerusalem of the North." Many refugees, arriving in Lithuania, believed that they had found a place where they could be free.

Storm Clouds

Unfortunately, Lithuania was not quite the haven it appeared to be. Although many of the refugees did not know it then, the Nazis were intent on taking over all of Europe. With the German army on the rampage, no place in Europe could be a true refuge. Even in Lithuania, Jews could not consider themselves safe from arrest, deportation, and murder at the hands of the Nazis. "In one moment," recalled Lithuanian-born Jew Solly Ganor of the war's outbreak, "I went from being a slightly spoiled, secure, normal boy to being a hunted animal."[5]

It was not the Nazis, however, but the nearby Soviet Union that first made inroads into Lithuanian government. The Soviets were eager to expand into Lithuanian territory; as a Soviet leader put it, "Lithuania . . . will have to join the glorious family of the Soviet Union."[6] Through 1939 and into 1940, the Soviets meddled more and more in Lithuania's internal affairs. Finally, in the summer of 1940, the Soviets annexed the entire country, making it a part of their empire.

Had the Soviets been as tolerant as the Lithuanians, the Soviet influence might have mattered little to the Jews of Lithuania. But that was not the case. The states that formed the Soviet Union had long histories of persecuting Jews. To be sure, the intolerance in these countries did not approach the atrocities committed by Germany under Hitler. "Better the Soviets than the Germans,"[7] Zev Birger's parents were fond of saying. Nevertheless, Jews throughout Lithuania distrusted the Soviets.

German sailors disembark on the shore of Memel, Lithuania, to enforce the Nazi occupation of the country.

As the Soviets moved in from the east, the greater menace of Hitler's army was pressing relentlessly forward. The Jews of Lithuania did not believe that the Soviets would protect them from the Nazi military; but no other protectors were in sight.

Passports, Visas, and Barriers

Although they had come seeking refuge, many Jews in Lithuania made the decision to leave the country by 1939 and 1940. This was no easy matter. Would-be travelers needed several documents. First and most basic was a passport. While most of the refugees had passports, some had lost theirs while fleeing to Lithuania. Others carried passports that were no longer valid. The countries that had issued them had been absorbed into the German empire and technically no longer existed.

For most Lithuanian refugees, though, documents called visas presented more complicated problems. Visas are permits issued by the country to which a person intends to travel. But very few countries were willing to issue visas to Jewish refugees. By mid-1940, the German army had already swept through much of the continent. Some

Pictured is a German passport issued in Nazi-controlled Poland. Jews had difficulty obtaining passports and visas once the Nazis occupied the countries in which they lived.

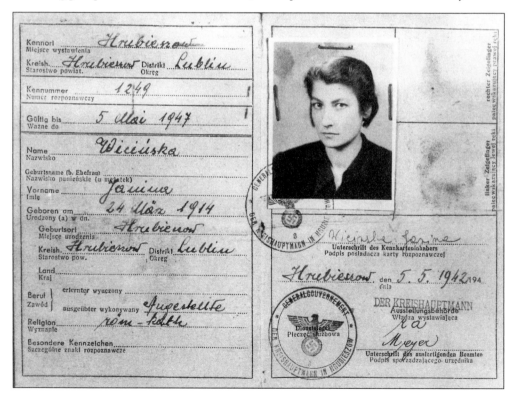

Nazi Supporters

The doctrines of Nazism often proved surprisingly popular in the countries occupied by the German army during World War II. Much of Europe was anti-Semitic and not necessarily opposed to the removal and oppression of the local Jews. While most Poles objected to German control of their country, for instance, quite a few approved of the anti-Semitic principles the invaders brought with them. The same was true in many other countries ranging from Slovakia to France. Jews who fled in advance of the Nazis were often running as much from the local populations as they were from the German army.

A crowd enthusiastically salutes Hitler as his car rolls through the street.

countries that had not yet been conquered were hard at work fighting the Nazis and had no resources to spare for refugees. Others, mainly those that remained neutral in the conflict, feared being flooded by Jewish immigrants. Most of Europe, then, was off-limits to Jews fleeing from Nazi persecution.

Countries on other continents were in a better position to take refugees. However, those nations issued comparatively few visas. The United States led the way by taking in about 132,000 European Jews during the period of Nazi power. But even that number was shamefully small compared with U. S. resources and the great need of Jews to leave Europe as quickly as possible. China took a few thousand; so did several countries in Latin America. Great Britain resettled some refugees in the British-held territory of Palestine in the

Middle East, but severely limited access to this region beginning in 1939.

Still, these countries were exceptions. Plenty of nations outside Europe accepted virtually no refugees at all. The reason, in most cases, was anti-Semitism. "We don't have a racial problem," explained an Australian official in a moment of honesty, "and we don't want to import one."[8] This official's attitude was all too common throughout the rest of the world. With few exceptions, the truth was that no one wanted the Jews.

The Search Intensifies

The Jewish refugees in Lithuania knew that the odds of finding visas were slim. But by the middle of 1940, there were no other options for escape. Nazi troops held most of the land west of Lithuania; it was senseless to try to escape in that direction. To the north lay Estonia and Latvia, two small nations no more likely to escape Nazi attack than Lithuania itself. To the south and the east lay the Soviet Union, a new nation with an old history of anti-Semitism. No Jew would flee Lithuania with the intention of making a home in any of the Soviet states.

But if Jews could not escape *to* the Soviet Union, it was at least conceivable that they might escape *through* Soviet territory. "We devoted time to plotting and planning how we might travel through Romania, Russia, and the other countries that lay between [Lithuania] and Palestine,"[9] remembered Zev Birger. Trains ran south to

Odessa, a Soviet port from which ships regularly departed for the Middle East. Trains also ran east to the Soviet city of Vladivostok on the Pacific Ocean. From there a Jewish refugee might be able to travel to the United States or Latin America. And while Soviet anti-Semitism could certainly be vicious, refugees would not fear for their lives simply by traveling across the country.

Indeed, many refugees hoped that Soviet officials might agree to allow them to pass through Soviet territory on a so-called transit visa. Transit visas did not allow a traveler to settle down in a country or even to remain there for long. They only permitted holders of the documents to pass through the country of issuance. If refugees had Soviet transit visas, then they had a possible escape route in the event of Nazi aggression.

But the Soviets were reluctant to give the refugees the documents they sought. Strongly anti-Semitic themselves, they did not want thousands of Jews arriving in the heart of the Soviet Union; instead, they were eager to restrict Jews to Lithuania and other areas on the outskirts of the Soviet empire. Thus, officials demanded assurance that the travelers had somewhere to go beyond the Soviet Union. Unless some other country offered permanent visas to the Lithuanian Jews, the Soviets decreed, the Soviet government would not issue any transit visas.

Visas, then, were the keys to escape. As time passed and the power of the Nazis grew, the search became ever

Ghetto police search and question a Jewish man. Anti-Semitism ran rampant throughout Europe and the Soviet Union before and during World War II.

more important. In the first half of 1940, more and more refugees set out on a frantic quest for visas.

Curaçao

They had little success, though, until a young student named Nathan Gutwirth discovered an odd loophole in the regulations. Gutwirth was a Dutch Jew living in Lithuania. Although his home country had been conquered by Germany, the Germans had not yet replaced all the Dutch diplomatic personnel in countries outside the Nazi orbit. Some of these posts remained in the hands of loyal Dutch who were forming a government in exile. Thus, in 1940, an anti-Nazi named Jan Zwartendijk was

running the Dutch consulate in the Lithuanian city of Kaunas.

Gutwirth knew that his country had a number of overseas possessions. Once a great naval power, the Netherlands had lost most of its colonies through the years. Nevertheless, it still controlled a few territories in the Caribbean Sea and South America. With the Nazis in charge of Holland, there was no reason for Gutwirth to return to his native country. But he thought it might be possible to travel to one of these colonial possessions.

Sometime in the summer of 1940, Gutwirth went to Zwartendijk and requested a visa for the Caribbean island of Curaçao. While looking through a set of regulations, Zwartendijk noticed that the wording of the visa for Curaçao differed from the wording of most other visas. Technically, in fact, the visa was not a visa at all, only an informal endorsement to be added to a traveler's passport. "For Curaçao," the document read, "no visa is required. Only the local Governor has the authority to issue landing permits."[10]

The first sentence of the document opened up interesting possibilities. If no visa was required, then Gutwirth—and anyone else who asked—could leave Lithuania on the strength of this endorsement alone. Unfortunately, the document's second sentence made the process much more complicated. Acceptance of the refugees would be at the discretion of the island's governor, who was under no obligation to let travelers in. Thus, other countries would be reluctant to let the refugees pass through their borders. Should Curaçao's gov-

The *St. Louis*

One of the saddest chapters in the history of anti-Semitism involves the journey of a ship called the *St. Louis*. The ship left Germany for Cuba in the spring of 1939, a few months before the outbreak of war. It carried 936 passengers, nearly all of them Jews and all holding visas allowing them to settle in Cuba. The mood on the ship was one of excitement and relief: The passengers thought they had successfully escaped Hitler and his anti-Jewish policies.

But when the ship arrived, Cuban customs officials refused to honor the visas the passengers presented. The Cuban government had changed its mind. Fueled by greed and ethnic prejudice, government leaders demanded a payment of 1 million dollars to allow the passengers to disembark. The Jews on the ship could not meet this price, even with help from Jewish organizations in the United States; and in early June the *St. Louis* steamed out of the harbor with all passengers still onboard.

The Cubans were not the only villains, however. Together with their American friends and relatives, the refugees appealed to the U.S. government. But the United States also declined to accept the refugees, even though the ship passed within a few miles of Florida. American Jewish organizations asked other Latin American countries for help, too, among them Paraguay, Argentina, and Colombia, but all refused.

The *St. Louis* had no choice but to return to Europe. There it discharged its passengers among four western European nations that agreed to take them. Unfortunately, three—Belgium, France, and the Netherlands—were soon conquered by the Nazis. The passengers of the *St. Louis* had thought themselves lucky, but the sad truth was that less than one in three survived the war.

ernor refuse the refugees admission, then they would be the responsibility of whatever government had them last.

On Gutwirth's behalf, Zwartendijk appealed to his superior, the Dutch ambassador in nearby Latvia. After much thought, the ambassador made a policy change. Zwartendijk, he ruled, could drop the second sentence altogether and stamp an applicant's passport with the first sentence alone. Henceforward, passports for travelers could state simply that no visa was required to enter the Dutch Caribbean.

Joining Forces

Word of the Dutch ambassador's decision spread quickly through the Lithuanian Jewish community. Within days, Zwartendijk's office was overwhelmed with refugees of all nationalities eager to obtain documents for Curaçao and other Dutch colonial possessions. "There was a long line leading to the front door [of the consulate]," remembered refugee Mojsze Grynberg. "I quickly climbed up [a water] pipe and entered the window. [Zwartendijk] looked a bit surprised but quickly issued me a visa."[11] Through July and into early August, Zwartendijk was kept busy drawing up documents for those who wished to escape Europe altogether.

To expedite Zwartendijk's handling of the requests, several refugees created rubber stamps bearing some of the necessary information. To expedite it still further, other refugees helped him stamp and organize the documents. Soon, operations at the small consulate had taken on the appearance of an assembly line, with Zwartendijk and his helpers efficiently processing the requests of hundreds of hopeful escapers.

However, the refugees' celebration was premature. Soviet officials soon announced that they would not issue transit visas to those who held endorsements for Curaçao. The Caribbean colony was simply too obscure, too small, and too distant. The Soviets suspected that the endorsements were not truly valid. Besides, there was no way to reach Curaçao directly from Soviet territory; if the next country in line refused to let the refugees pass, then the Jews would once again be the responsibility of the Soviets. Zwartendijk's visas would need to be supplemented by documents from closer, better-known countries before the Soviet government would allow passage to the refugees.

Once more, Lithuania's Jews responded. Zorach Warhaftig, a Polish Jew active in the refugee community, asked the British consulate for assistance. Britain had been reluctant to help before; now, for reasons that are unclear, officials decided to issue documents good for travel to Palestine. Again, the Jewish community offered its help in processing the documents. "The consul provided us with official stationery," remembered Warhaftig, "which we proceeded to fill in as required. We even appended the signature of the consul . . . may he forgive the impertinence!"[12]

The British assistance was invaluable. Unfortunately, it was short-lived.

Chiune Sugihara issued transit visas to Lithuanian Jews despite the danger of losing his job or his life.

Because of the Soviet takeover of Lithuania, the British were already in the process of shutting down their consulate there. Within a week after first offering safe passage, the British were gone. Worse yet for the Jews, at the same time Soviet authorities forced Zwartendijk to close down his own operation. Those in Lithuania who had already received the endorsements for the Dutch Caribbean could keep them; but

they still had no way out, and now there was no legal way for others to obtain the passes.

The Nazis continued to plow through Europe. The Jews of Lithuania were growing increasingly desperate. But Zorach Warhaftig was not ready to give up. He had already convinced British consular officials to provide him and his people with documents allowing them to escape from Lithuania. Now he would simply have to find another diplomat from a powerful country and convince him to do the same.

Chiune Sugihara

Warhaftig soon found a Japanese diplomat named Chiune Sugihara. Sugihara had opened the first Japanese consulate in Lithuania only a year earlier. A sophisticated and well-traveled man, Sugihara had kept a low profile in Lithuania. Before the summer of 1940, indeed, his name was scarcely known within the Jewish community. But in early August, Sugihara suddenly represented the last hope for the Jews of Lithuania.

On the surface, Sugihara seemed a very unlikely person to be assisting the refugees. For one thing, his country was friendly with Hitler's Germany; by 1941, in fact, the nations would fight together as allies. For another, Sugihara was not in Lithuania solely to serve as consul. His work as a diplomat was mainly a cover for his real assignment: collecting information on Soviet activities for the Nazis and their Japanese sympathizers. Sugihara, in short, was a pro-Nazi spy.

But Lithuania's Jews had no notion of Sugihara's political leanings. Warhaftig knew only that Japan was exactly the kind of place he was looking for: a strong and influential nation geographically close to the Soviet Union. If Sugihara could be persuaded to offer the refugees visas to Japan, Warhaftig believed, then the Soviets would allow them passage across their country.

Warhaftig and other leaders of the Jewish community decided that they would not ask Sugihara for regular visas. Their goal was simply to leave Lithuania; and for that purpose, a Japanese transit visa would work just as well. Such a visa would assure the Soviets that the travelers would have somewhere else to go. Besides, the Jewish leaders thought, Sugihara might be able to issue transit visas without checking with his superiors in Tokyo. If the plan worked, the refugees could deal later on with the question of finding permanent homes.

"We Will Be Killed"

One morning in early August, a group of Jewish refugees gathered outside the small Japanese consulate. Warhaftig had hoped that the gathering would arouse Sugihara's curiosity, and he was right. Puzzled, Sugihara summoned Warhaftig upstairs to his office and asked him what was going on.

Warhaftig was prepared. "We are Jews from Poland," he explained. "We will be killed if the Nazis catch us." He had brought a world map, which he unrolled on Sugihara's desk. "We have visas for Curaçao," he added, pointing out the island in relation to Lithuania, the Soviet Union, and Sugihara's own country. "Please give us transit visas that will permit us to travel [there] through Japan."[13]

Although he had arrived in Lithuania only recently, Sugihara was aware of the political issues in the country. He also knew the dangers faced by the local

An Early Promise to Help

Exactly when the plight of Lithuania's Jews came to Sugihara's attention is unclear. While most sources suggest that he became fully aware of the issues in the summer of 1940, perhaps somewhat earlier, at least one eyewitness argues that Sugihara's first exposure to the Jews' situation came soon after his arrival in Kaunas.

According to a story told by the Lithuanian Jew Solly Ganor, Sugihara attended a Hanukkah party at Ganor's family home in Kaunas late in 1939. There, he heard firsthand testimony from several Polish Jews who had come to Lithuania as refugees. Although Ganor was still a boy at the time, he recalls that Sugihara was deeply moved by these accounts. "I had no idea that the Germans were acting in such a despicable manner," Sugihara remarked, as quoted in Hillel Levin's *In Search of Sugihara;* and he promised to do what he could to help the refugees.

Jews, both from the Nazis and to a lesser extent from the Soviets. Indeed, Sugihara had already issued a few transit visas to those who had asked for them. As early as the spring of 1940, for example, he had helped a dissident Polish couple escape by giving them Japanese documents.

Sugihara was deeply moved by Warhaftig's request. In talking with Warhaftig and other Jewish leaders, Sugihara realized just how desperate the refugees' situation actually was. A few visas here and there would not do much to save the Jews of Lithuania. To be of help, Sugihara realized, he would have to do much more than he had been doing thus far.

Over the next few days, Sugihara wrestled with his conscience. On the one hand, he had to consider his career. While he was indeed empowered to issue transit visas, he doubted that his government would approve of him stepping up his efforts. He could easily lose his job, possibly even be jailed. The Nazis who hired him to spy might be angry, too—and if they chose to take retribution, there was a chance Sugihara might even lose his life. On the other hand, the people who assembled outside his consulate each day were definitely in need. "Among them were women, old people and children," Sugihara remembered nearly thirty years later. "They all seemed very tired and exhausted."[14]

The process of deciding took its toll. "For two whole nights," Sugihara wrote afterwards, "[I] was unable to sleep."[15]

But on August 10, 1940, Sugihara made up his mind. He informed Warhaftig that he would issue transit visas to anyone who held endorsements for Curaçao—and even extended the courtesy to those who did not. It would be possible to escape from Lithuania with the odd combination of a Curaçao endorsement and a visa to travel through Japan. Time was of the essence, and the Jews were in serious danger. Under the circumstances, Sugihara decided to

Nazi soldiers detain a Jewish man. Jews in Lithuania fled the country to avoid such persecution.

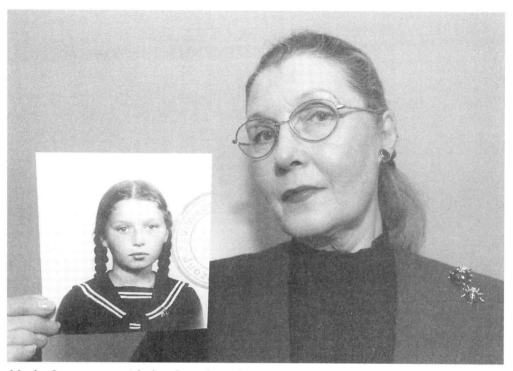

Masha Leon poses with the photo from the exit visa Chiune Sugihara issued to her in the early 1940s.

break the rules to get the refugees out quickly.

Exodus

Sugihara's statement far exceeded anything Warhaftig and the other refugees could have expected. Immediately, it seemed, hundreds of refugees descended on the small consulate in Kaunas. If Sugihara could be believed, it would now be possible for practically any Jew to leave the country, regardless of the validity of his or her documentation.

Most applicants, indeed, did not have legal permission to enter any other country at all. For that matter, some lacked documentation entirely. It was common for refugees to arrive at the consulate with obviously forged visas, without visas at all, or even without passports. But Sugihara's policy was to pass everyone through. In one typical case, a Polish Jew named Ludvik Salomon showed Sugihara a visa issued by the United States. The visa had long since expired, but Sugihara issued Salomon a Japanese transit visa regardless. "He issued transit visas to anyone who applied," sums up historian Hillel Levine, "whatever documents they presented or whatever explanation they gave for not having the right documents."[16]

After August 10, Sugihara spent virtually all his waking hours stamping passports. At first his only assistance came from his secretary, a sympathetic German named Wolfgang Gudze. But like Zwartendijk, Sugihara soon acquired rubber stamps to speed up the process. Several refugees volunteered their services, too. After Moshe Zupnik received his visa, for instance, he stayed on to expedite the claims of others. "For the next two weeks," he reported, "I used to come in and sit in the room . . . with Gudze. I was stamping and he was stamping."[17]

For many of the refugees, Sugihara's involvement seemed nothing short of a miracle. The British had abandoned them; the Soviets had not only refused any help but had forced the refugees' Dutch protectors to stop giving them assistance. Many Jews had been ready to give up when this unknown diplomat had unexpectedly offered them hope. "Half a century later," writes Levine, "[the refugees] didn't even know his name; they thought of him as an angel."[18] During the summer of 1940, the Jews of Lithuania besieged this "angel" for help, and he was happy to oblige.

Unfortunately, the miracle could not go on forever. Although the Soviets did issue transit visas for those who could produce Japanese documentation, they made it clear to Sugihara that they were not happy with the situation. The Japanese government was displeased, too, though not to the extent that Sugihara had feared: Their main objection was that Sugihara was not keeping his superiors informed. Whether the Nazis took steps to stop Sugihara is unknown. At the end of August, in any case, the Japanese closed the consulate in Kaunas and ordered Sugihara to a posting in Berlin. According to several sources, Sugihara continued to sign visas for Jewish refugees up until the moment the train pulled out of the station.

Aftermath

Once they had permission to leave, few Jews remained in Lithuania for long. Most immediately headed east, often leaving most of their possessions behind. Nearly all found the trek across the Soviet Union long, grueling, and tense; some were robbed or beaten by Soviet citizens or officials. But most did make it to Vladivostok, where they boarded ships for Japan.

From Japan the refugees spread out across the world. Many, perhaps most, made their way to China, where the validity of Sugihara's transit visas helped to win them asylum. Others found refuge in the United States, Latin America, or Palestine. Most had to undergo weeks or months of anxiety while they waited to see if the country of their choice would accept them. Still, they were out of Lithuania and away from the Nazis, not to mention the Soviets; and to most of them, that was what mattered.

One country, rather ironically, that got no refugees at all was the island that sparked the whole escape: Curaçao. Not a single refugee seems to have reached the small Dutch territory, let alone applied for asylum there. Indeed, many years later Warhaftig asked the former governor of the island whether he would have allowed the refugees into his country. "By no means!" replied the governor. "I would have made the ship put to sea again."[19] In light of this comment, it is clear that Sugihara's help was absolutely essential in allowing the refugees to escape.

Those who got out were the lucky ones. In 1941, the German army marched into Lithuania and exterminated nearly all of Lithuania's Jews. By 1945, there were scarcely more than one thousand left in the entire country. Virtually all the Lithuanian Jews who survived the war left during that hectic summer of 1940. Hillel Levine esti-

mates that Sugihara's documents saved perhaps ten thousand Jews and other refugees. Perhaps another few thousand made it out on documents issued by the Dutch or the British. The flight from Lithuania was massive and essential to the refugees' survival.

The credit for the escape goes to many different people, not least to the escapers themselves: the Jewish refugees who headed east into enemy territory in hopes of leaving the Nazis far behind. Still, much of the credit must go to Chiune Sugihara, the diplomat whose willingness to issue transit visas helped save the lives of thousands of people. "Who knows?" muses Hillel Levine. "If there had been a thousand Sugiharas, or a hundred, or perhaps only ten, perhaps there would not have been a Holocaust."[20]

2

Escape from Auschwitz

MOST OF THE people who escaped from Nazi persecution had seen for themselves just how brutal and uncompromising the Nazis could be. Thus, when an opportunity to flee presented itself, they took it. Whether running from a ghetto, a concentration camp, or simply from an increasingly oppressive atmosphere, these men, women, and children were motivated by the will to survive.

A handful of people who escaped the Nazis, however, had an additional motive for running away. These victims of Nazi persecution viewed their own survival as a means to a greater end: telling the world the truth about Nazism and the Holocaust. Perhaps the most important of these escapes was carried out in 1944 by Rudolf Vrba and Albert Wetzler, two Slovakian Jews imprisoned in the concentration camp at

Auschwitz, Poland. While their escape to safety was certainly dramatic, its aftermath was just as compelling. Their flight to freedom brought the world its first reliable information about the horrors of the Nazi concentration camp system.

Concentration Camps

The Nazi government carried out killings on a scale almost impossible to imagine. Nowhere was this evil more apparent than in the concentration camps of the German empire. Originally established to hold political prisoners and other "undesirables," the camps took on another purpose soon after World War II began: They became elaborate killing machines. Millions of camp inmates were gassed, shot, or otherwise put to death by their Nazi oppressors. At some of these camps, including Auschwitz, Nazi officials murdered tens of thousands of people every day.

The brutality of the concentration camps was astonishing. So was the cold-blooded efficiency with which Nazi leaders carried out their destruction. Worst of all were the sheer numbers: millions upon millions of people murdered, in most cases for no crime other than their ancestry. There had been events in world history which matched the Holocaust for its brutality, but few had approached its degree of hatred, its organization, and most of all the breadth of its impact. The world had never experienced anything quite

like the exterminations carried out by the Nazis.

That fact helped the Nazis keep their operations secret from the rest of the world. It seemed inconceivable that a nation would carry out murders on such a scale. From time to time, rumors spread that Auschwitz and other camps had become much more than prisons. But most who heard the stories discounted them, and the Nazis relied on that reaction. "After the war," Nazi soldiers at one concentration camp told a survivor, "the rest of the world [will] not believe what happened."[21]

For that matter, the Jews of Europe were themselves reluctant to believe the

Male prisoners await their demise at the Mauthausen concentration camp in Austria. Like at Mauthausen, tens of thousands were slaughtered at Auschwitz every day.

stories. "There had been certain rumours about the horrible events in Auschwitz," admitted Oscar Neumann, a leader of Jews in Slovakia. "But they were flying about like bats at night, they were not tangible."[22] And even those who arrived at the concentration camps often did not know what was happening to them. Most who arrived at Auschwitz, for instance, had been told that they were being resettled in another part of Europe. The rest were informed that they were heading to a work camp. "Although we didn't know where we were going," wrote inmate Wieslaw Kielar, "we didn't think it would be worse than prison."[23]

Auschwitz

They were wrong. The largest and probably most efficiently organized of all the Nazi concentration camps, Auschwitz was three camps in one. One section of the camp was used to hold political prisoners. A second section forced the inmates to labor as slaves on various work projects. But the third, sometimes known as Birkenau, was used strictly for extermination. During the course of the war, more than 1 million people were murdered in this camp by Nazis and their supporters.

The routine at the camp varied little from day to day. Trains arrived frequently, carrying with them prisoners from all over Europe. Most were immediately earmarked for extermination by the officials who ran the camp. Nazi guards sent them to a large basement room that resembled a changing area. There the new arrivals were instructed to remove their clothes and to walk

Jewish women and children who have been selected to die walk toward the gas chambers at Auschwitz in 1944.

down the hall to a communal shower room. The area was plastered with signs urging cleanliness, and guards even reminded people to remember where they had placed their clothing so they could pick it up afterwards.

But the instructions and the signs were a cruel sham. The faucets in the "shower rooms" were dummies; the rooms were actually gas chambers. Vents on the ceiling provided an entry point into the chambers for deadly cyanide gas, which would be piped in once the rooms were locked behind the victims. About a third of those in the chambers died as soon as the gas was released. The rest lived, but in agony, for up to twenty minutes before the gas did its work.

There was a reason why the victims were told that the chambers were really a shower room and why guards instructed new arrivals to keep track of where they had put their belongings. As Auschwitz inmate Filip Müller put it, "Every single detail was carefully aimed at allaying the victims' suspicions and calculated to take them quickly and without trouble into the gas chambers."[24] To let the victims know their fate in advance was to risk a riot or a rebellion. It was safer to have the inmates walk into the chambers of their own accord.

While most of the new arrivals were murdered within hours, the strongest and healthiest were put to work. The work was grueling and often pointless. "They would line us up every morning," recalled inmate Fritzie Fritshall, "and we would carry huge rocks from one side [of the camp] to another. . . .

The next day . . . we would take those same huge rocks, and we would carry them from that side back to this side."[25] Those who could not handle the workload were sent to the gas chambers.

Even for those who could manage the labor, however, life in Auschwitz was still utter misery. Nazi guards beat and occasionally killed inmates on the flimsiest of pretexts. Prisoners slept four or more to a bunk, often without blankets or mattresses. Food and water were scarce and often putrid, disease ran rampant through the camp, and human waste was everywhere. Some inmates lost their will to live; a few committed suicide. But most did what they could to survive a day at a time.

Vrba and Wetzler

Among the prisoners at Auschwitz were two Jews from the small country of Slovakia. Rudolf Vrba (who went at the time by the name of Walter Rosenberg, but later changed his name) had been deported to the camp in June 1942, when he was just seventeen years old. Alfred Wetzler, seven years older, had arrived at Auschwitz two months earlier. Because of their youth and health, they were each assigned to the labor camp upon their arrival.

Their jobs, however, were somewhat unusual for Auschwitz inmates. Vrba spent most of his first year at Auschwitz working as part of a so-called clearing commando. This work corps met almost all trains carrying prisoners to Auschwitz. Most of these trains had been packed tightly with men, women, and children, and many of those being transported had died on the way. Members of the commando pulled the corpses off the train; then they took the passengers' luggage, sorted it, and put it on a train for Germany.

Wetzler's job, in contrast, was both less strenuous and less emotionally draining. The Nazis kept careful records about many of their activities; thus, they needed clerical help. After his arrival at Auschwitz, Wetzler served as a registrar, or clerk, in several parts of the complex. He made lists, delivered papers, and wrote up bureaucratic reports for his Nazi overseers. In the summer of 1943, Vrba also became a registrar. Although the two men did not work on the same projects or in the same places, they nevertheless got to know one another through their shared experiences.

These jobs gave both Wetzler and Vrba unusual insight into the workings of Auschwitz. As registrars, they were privy to information generally kept away from inmates. Wetzler's work in various parts of the compound gave him a good sense of the prison's layout, and Vrba's earlier work with the commando showed him how the transport system operated.

It soon became clear to both Vrba and Wetzler that they knew more about

Prisoners who did not survive the journey to a concentration camp lay dead in a train car. One of Rudolf Vrba's jobs at Auschwitz was to help clear trains of people and luggage.

Human bones remain inside an Auschwitz crematorium oven. Wetzler and Vrba documented such atrocities and would later share their information with the world.

the camp than others. As they worked and observed, they realized that their positions gave them a special responsibility. They could be living testimony to the horrors of Auschwitz—horrors that still remained unknown to the world at large. Together, they vowed to somehow carry their information to the outside world so that millions would know the truth about the Nazis and the concentration camps.

To flesh out their own understanding of the camps, Wetzler and Vrba sought out others whose experiences of Auschwitz were vastly different from their own. The two talked to prisoners who served as skilled laborers and as members of construction crews; they

spoke with those who had been there for months and to those who had only recently arrived. They even talked to members of the so-called *Sonderkommando*, or special command, a group of prisoners assigned the appalling task of bringing the bodies of the murdered from the gas chambers to the crematoriums. The more Wetzler and Vrba talked to others, the more they knew.

Documenting this knowledge was dangerous. It was foolhardy for a prisoner to write anything down. A guard might grow suspicious if he saw an inmate committing something to paper. So Wetzler and Vrba memorized all that they saw and heard. Vrba memorized the points of origin for nearly every train that arrived in Auschwitz, along with the approximate number of passengers and their nationalities. Wetzler learned the dimensions of the camp. Both became walking encyclopedias, their minds filled with detailed knowledge of the camp and its structures.

Telling the World

As the years went on, Jews continued to pour into the camp. To Vrba and Wetzler it was obvious that the Nazis were carrying out a genocide—a deliberate extermination of an entire people—the likes of which the world had never seen before. Yet, so far as they could tell, no one on the outside knew it. Even the Jews sent to Auschwitz to be gassed did not know. None even appeared to suspect that 90 percent of those who arrived would be murdered within hours of their arrival.

It might have been possible for the registrars to let the newcomers know their fate as soon as they arrived. If they had, then perhaps a riot would have broken out; perhaps the prisoners on the transport would have fought back; perhaps some of the Nazi guards would have been injured or even killed. But the price for telling the new arrivals was high. Those who did alert the new arrivals were put to death in exceptionally brutal ways. One man, reported Filip Müller, "was pushed inside [a crematorium] and burned alive [while] the rest of us were made to watch."[26]

Nor would such a rebellion have had much chance of success. The exhausted,

Unloading the Transports

Years after his time at Auschwitz, Rudolf Vrba recalled the experience of meeting the transports as part of a work commando, as quoted in Claude Lanzmann's *Shoah: An Oral History of the Holocaust:*

Inside [the trains] there were people, of course, and you could see the people looking through the windows because they didn't know what was happening. They had many stops on the journey—some of them were ten days on the journey, some were two days on the journey—and they didn't know what this particular stop means. The door was opened and the first order they were given was "Alle heraus": "everybody out." And in order to make it quite clear, they usually started with [their] walking sticks to hit the first or second or third [passengers]. They were like sardines in those cars. If they expected on that day four or five or six transports, the pressure of getting out from the wagons was high. Then they used sticks, clubs, cursing, etcetera.

To allay the suspicions of those who arrived, Vrba added, "Whenever a new transport came, the ramp was cleaned absolutely to zero point. No trace from the previous transport was allowed to remain. Not one trace."

haggard prisoners streaming off the transport would have been quickly overwhelmed by the well-armed Nazis. The people to tell, Vrba and Wetzler believed, were those who were not yet captive. But as long as the two men were imprisoned inside Auschwitz, it seemed impossible to explain the situation to those outside.

In early 1944, as part of his job, Vrba came upon documents which suggested that the Jews of Hungary were next on Hitler's list. Up to this point, Hungarian Jews had remained relatively untouched by Nazi aggression. Although Hungary was allied with Germany and the Jews of that country had few rights, they had not been subject to the roundups, deportations, and mass murder that had befallen so many other Jewish populations in Europe. Hitler's Final Solution, however, called for no Jews to remain alive anywhere. Thus, Hungary's Jews were now in grave danger.

Vrba could not bear thinking about the Nazis' plans. When the time came, he feared, the Hungarian Jews would go to their doom just as quietly and unsuspectingly as had those from so many other nations. But if Vrba could tell the Jews of Hungary the truth about the transports, he reasoned, perhaps they would not be so accepting of the situation. "Would anybody get me alive to Auschwitz if I had this information?" he asked years later. "Would thousands and thousands of able-bodied Jewish men send their children, wives, mothers to Auschwitz from all over Europe, if they knew?"[27]

The thought of saving the Jews of Hungary by telling the world the truth about the concentration camps galvanized Vrba, and it had the same effect on Wetzler. They had survived Auschwitz for nearly two years, and there was no telling how much longer they might be allowed to live. If they died, their knowledge would die with them. Together, they decided that it was time to plot an escape.

"Doomed from the Start"

To escape from Auschwitz, however, was almost unimaginably difficult. The camp was thoroughly patrolled by dogs and soldiers. A fence of electrified barbed wire surrounded the compound. Beyond that was a secondary barrier with ditches, more fences, and watchtowers manned by sharpshooters. Inmates were forced to line up for frequent roll calls so that guards could keep careful track of where they were. Except for a few clerks like Vrba and Wetzler, prisoners who were found outside the areas where they worked risked being shot on sight.

Not only was security tight, but the prisoners themselves were in no shape to run away. Nearly all were overworked, exhausted, and malnourished. Many were sick. Day-to-day survival in a place like Auschwitz was difficult enough, and few prisoners had enough mental or physical energy to plan and carry out an escape.

But throughout the years of Auschwitz's operation, a surprising number of bold and ingenious inmates had found ways of getting out. By some counts, as many as 650 prisoners managed to escape. Most were quickly caught, but others were not. A man named Siegfried Lederer, for example, made a successful escape with the unexpected help of a Nazi corporal; he eventually joined freedom fighters in Slovakia and Poland. On another occasion, three Russian prisoners of war somehow joined a work crew assigned to labor outside the walls of the prison; once outside, they simply walked away.

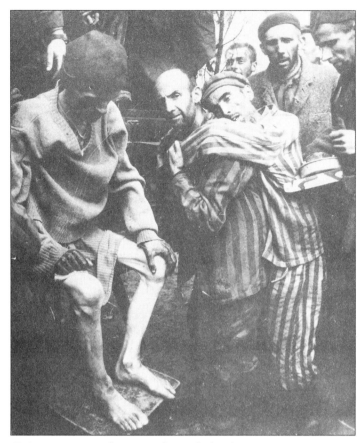

Prisoners struggle to get through the day at a concentration camp. Few prisoners attempted escape because most did not have the strength to run away.

The punishment for failure, however, was grim. Those who were captured while trying to flee were imprisoned in dark, cramped cells. "Breathing was almost impossible," wrote a Nazi who had visited the cells. "It was out of the question to sit down. Prisoners cowered in the darkness."[28] Inmates who had broken minor rules could be sentenced to these cells for days at a time, but those who tried to escape were left there to die.

Moreover, when someone escaped the Nazis usually took revenge against the other prisoners. Guards commonly shot a certain number of inmates for every prisoner who successfully ran away. Partly for this reason, some of the leaders among the prisoners actively discouraged escape efforts. These leaders—some Jewish, others Russian prisoners of war, and still others German political prisoners—had formed a small but vital resistance movement within the camp. They advocated mass violence against the Nazi guards and discouraged escape, which they called an "anarchic and individualistic activity."[29]

Vrba and Wetzler understood the resistance leaders' opposition to escape. Neither wished to put anyone in harm's way. At the same time, they believed it was better to alert the world to the true story of the camp—even at the risk of a few lives. In March 1944, they approached David Szmulewski, one of the leaders of the resistance group, and formally asked for permission to undertake the escape.

As Vrba had expected, Szmulewski turned them down. "Due to my inexperience . . . impulsiveness, and other factors," wrote Vrba many years later, "the leadership dismissed my intentions as unreliable."[30] But at the same time, Szmulewski let Vrba and Wetzler know that they could do what they liked, so long as they kept quiet about the resistance movement if caught. The leaders' opposition to escape was muted by their recognition of the need to let the world know the truth about Auschwitz.

A Secret Hideout

Vrba and Wetzler soon devised a plan for their flight. They knew they would need plenty of help, and so they judiciously spread the word among their fellow inmates, looking for those who might be willing to provide assistance. They found quite a few who were eager to help, including several who were part of a new work crew recently formed to build an extension to the prison.

"With the Utmost Severity"

Although the walls and guards of Auschwitz made escape extremely difficult, they were not the main reason why inmates did not make the attempt. The larger issue, for most, was what would happen once they got out. Most had lived far from the site of the camp; most of them had seen their neighborhoods and villages destroyed.

Additionally, few could expect any significant help from local populations if they did try to make their way home. Not only was there widespread anti-Jewish sentiment in eastern Europe, but Nazi Germany had strict rules applying to those who assisted Jews. A 1941 directive issued by a German governor of Warsaw read as follows, quoted in Mordecai Paldiel's book *The Path of the Righteous:*

> Any Jew who illegally leaves the designated residential district will be punished by death. Anyone who deliberately offers refuge to such Jews or who aids them in any other manner (i.e., offering a night's lodging, food, or by taking them into vehicles of any kind, etc.) will be subject to the same punishment. . . . I forcefully draw the attention of the entire population of the Warsaw District to this new decree, as henceforth it will be applied with the utmost severity.

This extension was located in an area nicknamed "Mexico" by Auschwitz's inmates. Mexico was a sort of a no-man's-land. While it was inside the fence that marked the outermost boundaries of the camp, it was outside the electrified barbed wire that formed Auschwitz's inner wall. Each day, dozens of laborers marched out through the barbed wire to the construction site, held back from freedom by dogs, guards, and ditches—but by only one fence. It was the opportunity Wetzler and Vrba had hoped for, and they took full advantage of it.

During the first few days of April 1944, the laborers at Mexico worked on their construction project as usual. From time to time, though, they would wander over to a pile of discarded lumber in the area. Any guard who noticed would simply have seen men innocently rooting through the woodpile. But in fact, they were hard at work digging a foxhole in the shadow of the lumber— a hole large enough to hold two men.

Late on the afternoon of April 6, Vrba and Wetzler used some pretext relating to their work as clerks to venture out into the construction site. When no one was looking, they ducked into the hole the crew had secretly dug for them. Quickly, several men from the work crew covered the hole with wooden boards and then scattered earth over the top. The camouflage was effective. Even up close, the hole looked like ordinary ground.

But the Nazis kept guard dogs, too, and the layers of board and soil would not mask the scent of the two men hidden below the earth. Vrba and Wetzler had discussed the situation with some Soviet prisoners of war, however, who had told them a trick. A mixture of tobacco and gasoline, they explained, would overpower a dog's sense of smell and make it impossible for it to pick up the odor of a person. The runaways followed the advice. The workers spread gasoline (which they probably stole from one of the work areas) near the area and added some shreds of tobacco. Then they left, leaving Vrba and Wetzler curled tightly in their underground bunker.

The Search

Vrba and Wetzler knew they would be easy to spot if they crossed the last barriers by day; but that was not why they stayed in the pit. In fact, they had no intention of trying to make a sudden break for freedom. Their two years in Auschwitz had taught them exactly how the Nazis reacted when a prisoner tried to make an escape. In their experience, trying to make a sudden break for freedom would be nearly suicidal.

They were well aware of the tight control the guards kept on the camp. Roll calls were frequent and thorough. Guards checked each group of prisoners several times a day and reported any absences immediately. Thus, it would be impossible for Vrba and Wetzler to get a decent head start. Their absence would be noted within an hour or two. Indeed, shortly after climbing into their bunker,

Another Escape Attempt

One of the best-known escape attempts from Auschwitz was carried out in July 1944 by two young inmates, Mala Zimetbaum and Edek Galinski. Zimetbaum was from Belgium, Galinski from Poland. The two fell in love and decided they would risk their lives in order to reach freedom together.

In the spring of 1944, Galinski managed to obtain pieces of a Nazi policeman's uniform. On July 24, Galinski dressed in the uniform and brought Zimetbaum out into the main courtyard of the prison camp. He told anyone who asked that Zimetbaum was being transferred to another camp, and that he had been selected to accompany her. Perhaps because there were fewer guards than usual that day, no one challenged him. The two walked successfully out of the main gate of the prison. They were free.

The story of Mala and Edek became well-known among the prisoners at Auschwitz. Many had known about their plans in advance; most found it romantic, inspiring, and dramatic. Unfortunately, theirs was not a happy ending. The Nazis soon noticed their absence and sounded an alarm. Within a few days the two were apprehended at the Czech border. They were returned to the camp and put to death. Nevertheless, their story helped give the prisoners of Auschwitz hope.

Wetzler and Vrba failed to line up with the other inmates at the evening roll call. Immediately, the guards raised an alarm.

Auschwitz was suddenly in turmoil. Sirens blared across the camp, alerting the staff that prisoners were on the loose. Off-duty guards seized their weapons and surrounded both the inner wall and the outer fence. The sharpshooters in the watchtowers doubled their concentration as they stared out over the darkening camp. Bright lights flashed throughout Auschwitz. Some soldiers searched the barracks, the offices, and the construction site. Others combed the nearby forests. "All through the night," wrote inmate Filip Müller, "the furious barking and yapping of the dogs could be heard."[31]

But the night passed without any of the guards finding a trace of the two men. So did the next day, and the next as well. The Nazis simply could not locate the escaped prisoners. Even their searches of the construction site came up empty. The laborers had left no obvious signs of fresh digging when they covered the foxhole. And the Soviet prisoners had been right; the mixture of tobacco and gasoline had indeed interfered with the dogs' sense of smell.

For three days in all, Vrba and Wetzler lay in their underground bunker. They had no way of knowing exactly what was going on above them. Like Müller, they could hear the barking of the dogs and the shouts of the Nazi soldiers; but unlike the other prisoners,

Vrba and Wetzler could not see any-thing that was happening. A sneeze, a cough, a sudden movement could give them away. They huddled together in the darkness, and they waited.

At last, on the evening of April 10, the camp commander called out, "Vacate guard posts!"[32] The order meant that the Nazis had officially giv-en up the search. Perhaps the escaped prisoners had somehow managed to get away, or perhaps they had died in the attempt; none of the guards could be sure. However, it seemed futile to con-tinue the security alert. The Nazis and their dogs had covered nearly every inch of the area inside and just outside the camp, and Vrba and Wetzler were nowhere to be seen.

Within an hour or so life at Auschwitz returned to normal. The dogs were brought to their kennels, and the soldiers at the fences went back to their usual du-ties. At ten o'clock that night Vrba and Wetzler emerged from their bunker, making sure they were not being ob-served. Then they crept toward the out-er fence of the compound. No one was visible but an occasional guard posted in the watchtowers. Moving slowly and cautiously, the men slipped through the fence and across the ditches that served as the outermost barrier of Auschwitz. No one stopped them. They were free.

South to Slovakia

Wetzler and Vrba now turned their sights to the south. Their intention was to travel to Slovakia, their na-tive country, where despite Nazi

Wetzler and Vrba knew they were free after they slipped through the final fence of Auschwitz.

oppression the Jewish community had not yet been completely destroyed. The two men knew that there was a Jewish organization active in the capital city of Bratislava. Eventually, they hoped to reach Bratislava to inform the council of the truth about Auschwitz. The first step, though, was to reach Slovakian territory some thirty or forty miles to the south.

Although they had escaped from Auschwitz itself, their struggles were far from over. Vrba and Wetzler were planning to travel through southern Poland, a Nazi-occupied country whose residents had little sympathy for Jews. Capture by either Nazi troops or local farmers could mean death. Moreover, Vrba and Wetzler were wanted men. The Nazis at Auschwitz, guessing that the pair had somehow pulled off an escape, had sent a telegram to nearby police forces alerting them to the runaways. "Request from you further search," the telegram read, "and in case of capture full report to concentration camp Auschwitz."[33]

Under ordinary circumstances, the journey south to the Slovakian border would have taken two or three days at the most. But Vrba and Wetzler did not dare take the easy route. In an effort to avoid encountering people, they traveled only at night. Likewise, they stayed away from the main roads and passed instead through forests and farmlands.

Spreading the Word

Rudolf Vrba and Alfred Wetzler were able to give the Slovakian Jews a remarkable array of information about Auschwitz and how it functioned. Oskar Krasnansky, one of the leaders of the country's Jewish movement, transcribed the data and had it typed. Then he sent copies of it to various places around Europe in hopes of spreading the information around Europe. Several of his reports were intercepted or otherwise delayed; one, sent to Turkey, fell into the hands of a Nazi sympathizer who gave it to the German secret police. Thus, word of the truth about Auschwitz traveled slowly from Slovakia.

In June 1944 a copy of the report reached neutral Switzerland. Those who read it were aghast. "We now know exactly what has happened," wrote a representative of a Jewish agency, quoted in Martin Gilbert's book *Auschwitz and the Allies*, "and where it has happened." Some urged the Allies to bomb the railroads leading to the camp. Others suggested destroying the camp itself, reasoning that most of those inside were doomed regardless. "Must delay not one day," read a telegram sent to the American government by a Jewish organization, also quoted in Gilbert's book.

But in the end these measures were not carried out. The Allies chose not to bomb Auschwitz or other concentration camps. They cited the cost and the danger of such a mission; they also argued that bombing the camps might infuriate the German leadership and make the situation worse. Today, though, many historians believe these were only excuses. Gilbert, like many others, blames the refusal to act on "Allied scepticism and disbelief" at the information they received from Vrba and Wetzler; he also attributes the decision to "political considerations and [anti-Jewish] prejudice." In any case, the bombings were not carried out, and through the remaining months of the war many thousands of Jews lost their lives in the death camp.

Escape Route of Vrba and Wetzler

GERMAN-OCCUPIED POLAND

GERMANY

Auschwitz

PROTECTORATE OF BOHEMIA-MORAVIA

Skalite

SLOVAKIA

Bratislava

GERMANY

The journey was grueling and perilous in other ways, too. The men had very little to eat, and their sleep was fitful at best. They had to rely on instinct and luck to keep heading in the right direction: As Vrba put it years later, they were "without documents, without a compass, without a map, and without a weapon."[34] Worst of all, despite their precautions, they were spotted at one point by a Nazi police patrol. The soldiers fired on them, but the pair managed to flee into the forest without being hit.

At last, on April 21, more than ten days after they had crawled out of their Auschwitz foxhole, Vrba and Wetzler found themselves back in Slovakia. Quite by accident they came across a friendly farmer outside the village of Skalite. "He was working in his fields," recalled Vrba. "He saw that we had crossed the border 'on our stomachs' [that is, sneaking in without papers] and

invited us for lunch."[35] It was a simple act of kindness, but a welcome one for two men who had seen very little generosity in the previous two years.

In the next few days, Vrba and Wetzler rested, ate their first full meals in months, and got in touch with the Jewish leaders in Bratislava. At the end of April, Vrba and Wetzler told their story to an attentive—and appalled—group of Slovakian Jews, who soon published the information and sent it across the world. Then the Jewish leaders gave Vrba and Wetzler false identities and sent them to a nearby town for their own protection.

Their escape was over. It had been dangerous, difficult, and frightening. Yet the hardships had been worth it, for Wetzler and Vrba had succeeded in doing what they had longed to do. For the first time, the world would know exactly what was going on inside the concentration camp at Auschwitz.

3

Escape from Colditz

DURING THE COURSE of World War II, many Allied soldiers were taken prisoner by the Nazis. Most were immediately put into special prison camps across Germany and its occupied territories. For soldiers from western Europe and North America, at least, these prisons were not nearly as bad as concentration camps. While there were always exceptions, these soldiers (and in particular, their captured officers) were generally not brutalized on a regular basis; they were not worked to the point of exhaustion; and there were no gas chambers awaiting them when they arrived at their prisons.

Part of the reason for this treatment involved an international document called the Geneva Convention. First written in 1864 and revised several times

thereafter, the Geneva Convention spelled out rules by which prisoners of war were to be treated. According to the document, countries had to meet certain standards in feeding, clothing, and housing their prisoners. The regulations forbade excessively harsh discipline as well, and prevented nations from using captured officers as laborers. Germany had signed the 1929 version of the document, and despite Hitler's brutalities, the Nazis did adhere to at least some degree to the Geneva Convention where prisoners from western Europe were concerned.

Nevertheless, the life of a prisoner of war was far from easy. Most soldiers, for instance, suffered from hunger, as the Germans gave them very little to eat. Supplies sent by the International Red Cross occasionally supplemented the prisoners' diets, but these packages arrived irregularly. Punishment for breaking camp rules, similarly, was usually unpleasant; offenders might be put into solitary confinement for weeks or even months. The prisoners hated being kept under constant watch by armed guards. And no one knew if Hitler would continue to abide by the rules set by the Geneva Convention.

It was no surprise, then, that some of these prisoners of war thought about escaping. The odds, however, were against them. Most of the prisons were designed for maximum security, and many were deep inside German territory; a man who managed to get outside the walls was still far from safety. Nevertheless, during the course of World War II a number of prisoners of war did carry out successful escapes. None of these were more ingenious or dramatic than a 1942 breakout from the high-security Colditz camp in eastern Germany.

Colditz

Colditz was a prison. It was also a castle. Originally constructed in 1014 as a fortress, Colditz had been remodeled and added to several times over the years. On various occasions it had been used as a hunting lodge, a home for the nobility, and a poorhouse. When Hitler came to power, the seven-hundred room edifice was being used as an asylum, but the Nazis quickly decided to convert it into a prison.

But Colditz was no ordinary prison. Most prisoners of war—officers and enlisted men alike—were shipped to Königstein, Spangenburg, and a host of other camps around Germany and its occupied territories. Colditz was set aside for officers, and a particular group

Prisoners of War

The Nazis dealt with prisoners of war, or POWs, very differently according to their national origins. While Nazi treatment of British, French, and American soldiers was often harsh and sometimes downright brutal, the Germans did for the most part adhere to the Geneva Convention where these men were concerned. Prisoners from eastern Europe, however, fared differently. That was especially true for soldiers from the Soviet Union. Many of these men were sent to concentration camps and dealt with much as Hitler treated the Jews; indeed, counts of the Holocaust dead sometimes include 3.3 million Soviet POWs.

While there were many reasons for the differing treatment, the most important involved Nazi racial ideas. To Hitler, northwestern Europeans such as the British were close to being Aryan. Slavs and other eastern Europeans, on the other hand, were nearly as undesirable to the Nazis as were the Jews.

Colditz Castle sits high atop a hill in eastern Germany. The building was originally constructed as a fortress in 1014.

of officers at that. Its population consisted mainly of men who had escaped from one of these other camps but had been recaptured before making it safely home. The few inmates who had not attempted escape had been unusually disobedient in their previous prisons. It was, as one inmate rather proudly described it, "the bad boys' camp."[36]

The Nazis imprisoned all these men together in Colditz because they believed the castle was the strongest and most escape proof of all their prisoner of war camps. Four stories high, Colditz had been built on a hill. Cliffs surrounded the castle on three sides; the remaining side was defended by a deep trench that had once been a moat.

The castle had strong stone walls, supplemented in places by barbed wire, and floodlights that illuminated the grounds night and day. The prisoners were confined to an inner courtyard; the outer courtyard, which led to the castle's only two entrances, was used exclusively by the Nazis. "From here," a guard boasted to an inmate, "there will be no escape."[37]

Strong as the castle was, it had its flaws. "Apart from putting bars on the windows," pointed out a German who worked as a security officer at Colditz, "[the prison] had never really been built for the purpose of keeping people *in*."[38] The castle was full of old doors, walled-off vents, and crumbling bricks, and it had too many rooms for the Nazis to monitor their prisoners at all times. For fending off attacks from outside, the castle was an effective fortress even as late as World War II. As a prison, however, it was not as ideal as Nazi officers believed.

The second flaw lay with the Nazis' decision to fill Colditz with officers who had already tried to escape. During World War II, comparatively few prisoners of war ever tried to flee their captors. Those who did were not representative of the prisoners as a whole. As a group, they were unusually daring and ingenious; most of all, they were enthusiastic risk takers. Once they were grouped together, these men reinforced each other's desire to escape—and shared techniques and ideas that had worked in the past. Unwittingly, wrote British officer Pat Reid, the Germans had "gathered together in one place . . . all the escape technicians of the Allied forces from all over the world."[39]

Picking Locks and Making Plans

The four hundred or so prisoners at Colditz indeed represented a variety of cultures. Many were British. A few came from Canada, Australia, or other former British possessions; one was from India. Colditz also held a large contingent of Polish prisoners of war, and other inmates came from the Netherlands, France, and Belgium. While the different nationalities stayed apart from one another at first for reasons of language and culture, they soon came together over the prospect of escape.

The inmates of Colditz took the possibility of escape very seriously. Among them, the men had made several hundred unsuccessful escape attempts from other prisoner of war camps, and nearly every inmate longed for another chance. Prisoners informally compared notes with one another: what their plans had been, what went wrong, what they had learned from their mistakes.

Activities and Diversions

Because the Geneva Convention forbade captured officers from working for the enemy, the prisoners at Colditz had very little to occupy their time. However, their Nazi guards were generally willing to allow them diversions. Although these activities could be canceled at any moment—and sometimes were—the inmates appreciated the opportunity to do something other than sit in their cells. Some men, for instance, played sports in the prison's cramped exercise yard. Others put on amateur theatricals or played an instrument in a small orchestra. While the men were not by any means allowed to do what they pleased, they did have a certain freedom of movement and action. This allowed them the time and space to manufacture the clothing and documents they would need for their escapes.

Soviet soldiers sit down to a meal in a prison camp. Colditz POWs were treated better than inmates of concentration camps.

As time went on, the inmates began to investigate the question of escape in more practical ways, too. Several Polish prisoners, for instance, realized that the locks on many of the castle's doors could easily be picked. They shared their secret with others, and soon few rooms of the prisoners' courtyard were off-limits to adventuresome inmates. Prisoners explored these rooms with an eye toward constructing tunnels to the outside, listening all the while for the sound of guards at the door. Other inmates learned everything they could about Colditz's layout, construction, and plumbing.

By early 1941, the inmates at Colditz had formed their own escape committee. This group of prisoners, with members drawn from each nationality in the jail, was charged with coordinating and evaluating escape plans. While it did not have any formal power to prevent inmates from escaping, it could advise against a prisoner making use of a particular scheme. To be successful, the committee believed, an escape attempt should involve no more than four to six people; it should be carefully thought-out; and it should have a reasonable chance of success. In the eyes of committee members, any other plan was not worth attempting.

Documents, Money, and Clothes

But hard as it would be to break through the castle walls, an escaped prisoner's greater challenge came in trying to reach neutral zones. Colditz was in eastern Germany, deep in the heart of Nazi territory. The closest friendly country was Switzerland, nearly four hundred miles away. Conceivably, a prisoner might be able to travel the distance in secret, moving through the woods at night, but the distance was so great that it was considered better to travel in disguise. Thus, a prisoner who escaped would need civilian clothing, money, and documentation; otherwise, he would be arrested and sent back to Colditz.

45

None of these items was easily available inside the prison, but the men of Colditz were not daunted. For clothing, they stole coats and hats belonging to the Germans who worked in the prison. They also set up workrooms in out-of-the-way parts of the castle. There, officers sewed and dyed bits and pieces of blankets, handkerchiefs, and other fabrics to approximate civilian outfits. Many of these items, recalled Pat Reid, "looked quite professional."[40]

Money was a different problem. The men of Colditz found the Red Cross food packages invaluable for this purpose. They offered the German guards some of the choicest morsels in exchange for a few marks, the German unit of currency. While some of the Nazis refused the offer, others accepted. Then the prisoners squirreled away the cash for use in a later escape. Of course, whenever possible, inmates also stole from the guards and other visitors to the jail, and some prisoners, especially those who lived in occupied territories, received German marks hidden in letters.

The most pressing issue, though, was documentation. Wartime Germany was a police state through which no one could travel without proper identification. The prisoners overcame this problem by manufacturing false documents. Inmates skilled in art and lettering copied genuine documents, taken secretly from guards and then replaced. The distinctive German script found on many of the identity cards used in Nazi territory proved relatively easy to imitate. Making handwritten copies of typewritten documents was much more difficult. Two Colditz inmates, however, had this talent; later

Colditz inmates who forged documents carefully imitated the typewriting of genuine identification cards like this one.

46

on, a Polish officer managed to construct a folding typewriter that did the job even better.

The making of forged documents was easier than it might have been, though, because Germany issued dozens of different identity documents. Foreigners of different nationalities had different documents; for that matter, native Germans could carry any of a number of papers. "Not even trained members of the Gestapo [the German secret police] could recognise all of them at sight," wrote one commentator, "and any authoritatively worded pass . . . was almost certain to survive examination."[41] A document merely needed to look official; it did not need to be a perfect forgery.

Failure

Through 1941 and into 1942, the prisoners at Colditz made many escape attempts. At times it seemed as if there was an escape every other day. The methods used by the men were inventive and often highly sophisticated. Many prisoners constructed tunnels, sometimes using no equipment sharper than a table knife; a few of these tunnels extended hundreds of feet. Another constructed a dummy to confuse the guards. One man put on a dress that he had painstakingly sewed, passed himself off as a female visitor to the prison, and attempted to walk through the gates.

The German guards knew they always had to be alert to the possibility of escape. The inmates of Colditz were seasoned escapers. Besides, they had little to do but to plot. "We were en-

gaged in a permanent game of leapfrog," wrote a Nazi official. "First we were ahead with our security barriers, then they were, scheming around them."[42] But despite the effort, very few of the escape attempts were successful.

Most of the time, in fact, the Germans were aware of the prisoners' plans almost from the start. That was especially true with plans that involved tunnels or disguise. Rather than stop the men immediately, though, the guards usually let them continue until it was almost time for the breakout. Then the Nazis swooped in and carted the prisoners off to solitary confinement. While a handful of inmates did successfully reach freedom, most prisoners who tried to escape never got past the outer walls. Many never even left the prisoners' courtyard. Still, the men of Colditz continued to think and to plan.

Through the Eye of the Needle

In the summer of 1942, two British officers, Billie Stephens and Ronnie Littledale, arrived in Colditz from other prisons. After briefly scouting the layout of the prison, they brought an escape plan to members of the committee. The newcomers' plan hinged on a quirk of the castle's layout. The kitchen where the inmates' food was prepared faced the prisoners' quarters in the inner courtyard. The back of the kitchen, however, was connected to the Germans' own kitchen, which in turn bordered on the castle's outer courtyard. Stephens and

Heinrich Himmler inspects a prisoner of war in Germany. Pat Reid understood how difficult it would be to escape from Colditz.

Littledale had noticed that the roofs of the two buildings were not even. The prisoners' kitchen was higher. In fact, it contained a window that looked out over the flat roof of the Nazis' kitchen.

For the two British officers, this represented a wonderful opportunity. A prisoner who could get into the inmates' kitchen could go out the window and onto the roof of the lower building. From there, it might be possible to drop down into the outer courtyard. Stephens and Littledale were not entirely certain where they would go after that. But as they reminded the members of the escape committee, that route would at least put them near the two main exits to the building.

At first, camp veterans were inclined to scoff at the newcomers' suggestion. "It has about as much chance of success as the famous camel that tried to go through the eye of a needle,"[43] remarked Reid when he heard the details. The problems seemed many and insurmountable. The prisoners' kitchen was off-limits during the day; floodlights were trained directly on the roof of the German kitchen by night. It seemed implausible that the sentries in the outer courtyard would fail to notice men dropping down from above. And most obviously, even the men who had thought of the plan had no idea how they would escape from the outer courtyard, assuming they ever got that far.

Yet in the end, the committee agreed to let the men try. Despite his misgivings, Reid even decided to join them. He invited a fourth man, too, a Canadian named Hank Wardle. For the next few weeks, the four men planned their escape, gathered the documents and clothing they would need, and rehearsed their new identities.

To the Courtyard

By October 14, everything was ready. The four prisoners met outside the inmates' kitchen at 6:30 P.M., soon after the final roll call of the day. Each wore civilian clothing and carried passes identifying them as foreigners living in Germany. Each man also carried a small suitcase. This was Reid's idea; although the suitcases might slow them down inside the castle, the props would help them look less suspicious once they were outside the prison.

Now that the day was over, the kitchen was empty. It was also locked, but that presented no problem to the four escapers. Reid had found an unlocked front window, and the men used this entry point to climb into the kitchen. In after-hours ventures into the kitchen earlier that week, Reid and some of his fellow prisoners had slowly loosened one of the bars on the rear window. Now they pried the bar completely off its

moorings, leaving a hole large enough for a man to squeeze through.

The roof of the German kitchen lay just beyond the windowsill. Reid quickly slid out the window and onto the long, flat roof, illuminated by the glare of three or four floodlights. "The eyes of a hundred windows glared down upon me,"[44] he wrote later. But luck was with him. No one was watching, either from the courtyard below or from the castle windows above. One by one, Littledale, Stephens, and Wardle followed. Making their way across the roof, the men dropped into the shadows of the outer courtyard.

The next step was to cross the courtyard. Reid hoped to reach the German

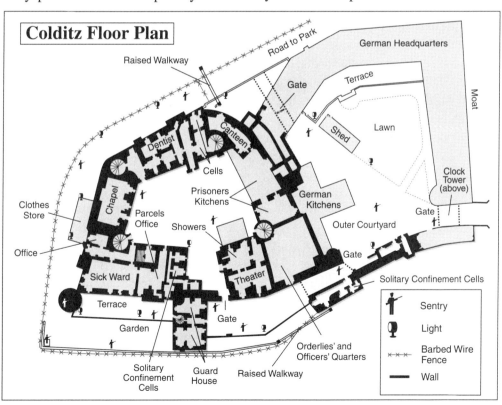

headquarters building, which bordered the moat. Unfortunately, getting across the open courtyard was an extremely tricky proposition. A German sentry patrolled the area all day and night, walking back and forth in an inconsistent pattern. "From where they hid," recalled a fellow inmate, "Pat and the others could not see the sentry."[45]

The escapers, however, had planned for this possibility. The guard was visible from some of the rooms in the prisoners' quarters. In particular, there was a small room on the third floor that had been used as a theater, and this room afforded inmates an excellent view of the sentry's movements. Early in their incarceration, a few prisoners had formed a small orchestra, which used the theater room to rehearse. Before escaping, Reid and his friends discussed their situation with the players and the conductor. Then they made sure that the orchestra would be practicing on the night they made their escape.

Their plan was simple. Beginning at eight o'clock, the conductor would stop the orchestra whenever it was safe for Reid and his friends to cross the courtyard. If music was playing, the men would take it as a signal to stay put. Unfortunately, the plot did not go as expected. The sentry's movements were simply too irregular. The music stopped, started, stopped, and started again, never giving the escapers a chance to get going. Worse, the constant starts and stops made the guards suspicious. They broke up the rehearsal and sent the musicians back to their cells.

Reid and his friends refused to panic. For the next hour they listened carefully to the sound of the sentry's boots against the castle's cobblestones. This information helped them determine when the man might be furthest away from them. At about 9:45, the four escapers seized their chance. One by one, they dashed across the floodlit courtyard and dived into a shallow pit next to the Nazi headquarters. No one stopped them. For the moment, they were safe.

"Like Toothpaste Out of a Tube"

Although the main gates of the castle were on the same side of the courtyard, the men believed they had no realistic chance of escaping through them. They hoped instead to find an overlooked route out the back of the German headquarters building, which formed part of the castle wall. Reid, a civil engineer, was convinced that there must be such a route; if nothing else, he argued, some of the castle's ancient drainage tunnels probably led to the outside.

In order to find a route out the back of the building, though, it was first necessary for the escapers to find a way in. The men tried to pick the lock of a workshop connected to the headquarters, but the lock would not yield. Working their way silently along the outside of the headquarters building, they eventually came to an unlocked cellar. It seemed at first as though the cellar led nowhere, but a faint light shone through the ceiling at the very back of the room. The men investigated and found an air vent about three-feet-wide and nine-inches-high.

Although the air vent was unpleasantly narrow, the presence of the light indicated that it might lead outside. Wardle boosted Reid up to the ceiling to take a look. The vent, Reid discovered, went up about four feet and then curved forward to end at an opening in the outside wall. But Reid's delight in finding a passage out of the castle was tempered by two other discoveries. First, the opening was covered by bars, and second, the passageway never got any wider.

The men soon decided that they had no reasonable alternatives. They stripped naked, making themselves as thin as possible in order to clamber through the narrow passage. Reid, a short and skinny man, went first. Despite his small size and agility, he nearly got stuck in the curve while his comrades watched from below. After much struggle, however, he successfully made it to the end of the vent. Only the bars still remained. As Reid had hoped, they were old and loose, and he slowly pulled them away from the nearby stone. Slipping through the hole, Reid dropped to the ground below.

With Reid safely out, the three other men passed the clothes and suitcases through the hole to Reid, and then set

Pat Reid (left), Alan Campbell (center), and Dick Howe recall their successful escapes from Colditz at a reunion in London in 1955.

Fooling the Nazis

The Nazis who guarded Colditz did their best to figure out how Stephens, Littledale, Wardle, and Reid had made their way out of the prison. They brought in guard dogs, who followed the men's scent to the cellar and the air vent that led outside. There, the guards noticed the bent bars at the end of the tunnel; they also discovered a few candy wrappers that the escapers had accidentally left on the ground.

Still, security officer Reinhold Eggers was unconvinced that the men had actually been there. Because he simply could not imagine that the men could have crossed the outer courtyard, he decided that the prisoners must have escaped some other way. The dogs' usually keen sense of smell, he believed, had been corrupted by a strong odor of sewage in the cellar. And the candy wrappers, Eggers was sure, had been left by a German guard taking an unauthorized break from his work. Only in 1952, when Pat Reid published the British edition of *The Colditz Story*, did Eggers find that he had been wrong.

to the task of escaping themselves. Wardle and Stephens were large men, and they struggled mightily to manage the curve. But Littledale pushed from inside and Reid pulled from the outside, and they inched forward. In the end, both men emerged from the tunnel, though it had been a close call. "[Wardle] was bruised all over and streaming with perspiration,"[46] remembered Reid, and Stephens was not much better off.

Littledale, the smallest of the four, went last. His escape required the least amount of time; even so, it took about ten minutes for him to make it safely outside the castle walls. Later, Reid would write that they had "squeezed through a hole in the wall, like toothpaste out of a tube."[47] The men dressed and contemplated their next move. Though beyond the castle walls, they were hardly home free.

The Last Barrier

The vent through which the men had escaped opened onto a narrow path running along the castle's moat. The slope down into the moat was sheer but not unmanageable; luckily for the men, it was split into three separate drops of about fifteen feet each. One of the suitcases contained a bedsheet that the men had brought along for just this purpose. Using the rolled sheet like a rope, they lowered each other down the side of the trench. Twice during the descent the men heard the barking of dogs, but the Germans seemed not to notice. By 4:30 in the morning the group had reached the bottom.

The other side of the moat, fortunately, was gentler. The climb to the top led the men to a path that snaked around the outside of a dormitory reserved for married guards and their wives. Now they walked as calmly and leisurely as possible, hoping that any observer would think they were sentries returning to their barracks after a long day of work. In fact, that deception was not necessary: No one noticed them.

Only one barrier remained: an outer wall, known as the "park wall," that separated the grounds of the castle from the German countryside below. The park wall was ten feet high and topped with barbed wire, but the men were too close to freedom now to be discouraged. As at the air vent, those on the bottom boosted their companions up, and those already further along helped by pulling. Even the coils of wire were not enough to stop the men for long. "The barbed wire," wrote Reid later on, "did not present a serious obstacle when tackled without hurry and with minute care."[48] Cautiously, the men eased themselves and each other around the barbs. By 5:15 A.M. all four were over the wall.

The journey to this point had covered a good deal less than a mile, but it had taken about eleven hours. Yet the men still had a long way to go. The freedom of Switzerland lay almost four hundred miles to the southwest. By no means could the men consider themselves truly safe.

"See You in Switzerland"

Outside the castle wall, the four men shook hands. According to their original script, they would now split into two groups and make their way separately to the Swiss border. Four men traveling together would probably at-tract attention; two men, on the other hand, would not. Wardle and Reid went one way, Littledale and Stephens the other. "See you in Switzerland,"[49] they whispered as they parted.

For both pairs, the first step was to get as far from Colditz as possible before stopping to rest. In just a few hours the Nazi guards would call the roll, and their disappearance would be noted. Every police officer in the area would be looking for them. Littledale and Stephens headed for the nearest train station to board a train scheduled to leave just before roll call would take

A German border guard checks a man's identification. The four escapees posed as Belgians to board a train in Germany.

place. Wardle and Reid, in contrast, hurried through the woods toward a more distant town, where they intended to catch a train themselves—but not for a day or two, after the commotion had died down.

Both groups found that their disguises worked well, and neither pair had any difficulty boarding the proper train. Although none of the men spoke particularly good German, they knew enough to carry out simple transactions. Moreover, they did not need to know much of the language. Their neatly forged identification cards marked them as Belgian citizens whose native language was Flemish, a tongue similar to Dutch. This strategy explained the men's poor German and mediocre French. At the same time the prisoners could be reasonably sure that they would encounter no one who actually spoke Flemish and could reveal them as frauds.

Despite the news of the escaped prisoners, no one accosted Wardle and Reid at the station when they began their journey. And as they made their way through the towns of southern Germany, all four men slowly began to relax. No one, it seemed, gave the travelers a second look. Even when Reid accidentally called out to Wardle in English at the Munich train station, no one came forward to arrest or question the men.

A major challenge lay ahead, however. The Nazis guarded the Swiss border with extreme care. While there was no fence or other barrier along the line that divided the two nations, the Germans had placed checkpoints at regular intervals along the border to keep people from escaping into neutral territory. Worse yet, the border curved frequently, making it difficult for travelers to know precisely where they were. In the previous year, several men of Colditz had made it all the way to the Swiss border only to be apprehended before they could cross to safety.

Over the Border

Although Stephens and Littledale had left Colditz by an earlier train, they had taken a more roundabout route. Wardle and Reid therefore arrived in the border region first. They got off a train at a village called Tuttlingen, about fifteen miles from Swiss territory, and decided to hike the rest of the way. Unfortunately, there were no signs directing them toward the border, and the men promptly got lost. It took most of a day to discover the correct road, and by then it was too late to go much further. Thus, they were forced to spend the night in the forest.

The next morning, October 18, the men set out again. They walked most of the day, keeping to the forests when they could and following the roads when they had to. Late in the afternoon, with less than a mile to go, they were suddenly stopped by a Nazi sentry who demanded their identification. Reid handed the man their passes. Doing his best to sound friendly, open, and somewhat vague, he explained in broken German that he and Wardle were foreigners enjoying the beautiful mountain scenery as they walked to a nearby town to look for work. The guard looked carefully at the two men, studied the passes—and then, to the soldiers' relief, waved them on.

As soon as Wardle and Reid were past the sentry, they left the road and hid once more in the forests. The two men decided they would be best off using darkness as a cover to travel the last

stretch into Switzerland. Quickly, they pulled an extra pair of socks on over their shoes, thereby muffling their footsteps. Next they buried their suitcases, which at this point would only slow them down. Then they set off silently through the forest.

This last dash to safety both excited and terrified Reid and Wardle. "Even the crackle of a dry leaf caused me to perspire freely,"[50] Reid admitted years

The "Great Escape"

While the escape carried out by Stephens, Reid, Littledale, and Wardle was certainly dramatic, it is not the best-known escape from Nazi prisoner-of-war camps. That honor probably goes to a 1944 breakout from a German camp called Stalag Luft III. The subject of a popular movie some years later, the attempt is widely known today as the "Great Escape."

Stalag Luft III was a much larger prison than Colditz. By 1943, there were roughly ten thousand prisoners at the camp. Late that year some of the inmates began trying to dig three tunnels to freedom. The plans for the tunnels, nicknamed Tom, Dick, and Harry, were complex. Because the Germans had listening devices that could pick up the sound of digging near the prison walls, the prisoners first had to dig down out of the range of the devices (about thirty feet in all) before they could begin to dig out. All the dirt and sand had to go somewhere, too, and the men smuggled it out of the tunnels in the legs of their pants.

The tunnel called Tom was found by guards and dynamited, but Harry was finished in early 1944. On the night of March 24, a group of two hundred men tried to crawl their way through the tunnel and into a patch of woods more than one hundred yards away. Their progress was interrupted by patrols and an Allied air raid, though, and by morning only seventy-six men had reached the safety of the forest. Worse yet, the last three were spotted by a Nazi sentry near the prison gates.

The escape set off an elaborate manhunt all across Germany and its occupied territories. It might have been possible for a small group of escapees to avoid detection, but there were simply too many prisoners on the loose for the Germans to ignore. Twenty-three men were quickly captured and returned to Stalag Luft III or other prisons. Fifty more were rounded up and machine-gunned to death; their escape had infuriated Hitler, and he was eager to send any other prospective escapers a message. Only three men of the seventy-six who reached the woods made it safely to neutral territory.

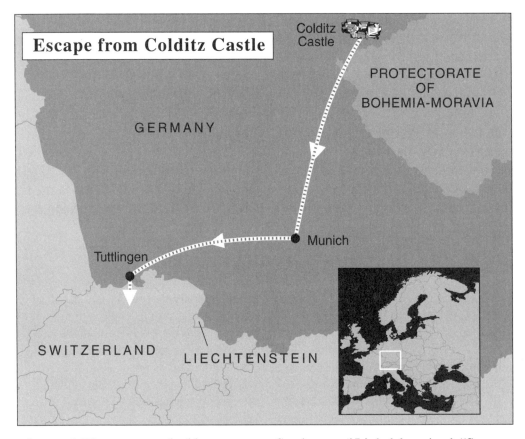

Escape from Colditz Castle

Colditz Castle

PROTECTORATE OF BOHEMIA-MORAVIA

GERMANY

Tuttlingen

Munich

SWITZERLAND   LIECHTENSTEIN

afterward. The men crouched low every time they saw a light or heard a noise, and more than once they lost their bearings. They were heading for a small Swiss village they knew lay somewhere in the region; but as Reid had feared, the curves of the border made it very difficult for the men to know which way to go. At one point the two came within five yards of a German guardhouse before they realized their mistake.

But the men kept their wits and headed grimly on. At 8:30 that evening, the two arrived at their destination. The following evening, exactly as planned, Stephens and Littledale arrived. "See you in Switzerland,"[51] the prisoners had told one another outside the gates of the castle; and they had done just that. No other World War II escape from Colditz was nearly as successful. All other escapes from the prison either involved fewer people or resulted in the capture of some of the escapers before they could reach safety. The flight of Stephens, Reid, Littledale, and Wardle was unique: Each of the four men made his way to safety. They had met each hardship with ingenuity and every setback with courage, and they won their freedom.

4

Out of Denmark

ALTHOUGH THE PEOPLE of many conquered European nations accepted some of the doctrines of Nazism, there were a few occupied countries where pro-Nazi sentiment was rare. Chief among these nations was the small Scandinavian nation of Denmark, just north of Germany. Unlike many other Europeans, the Danes resisted Nazism even as the Germans controlled their national affairs. They staunchly defended the eight thousand or so Jews who lived in Denmark. When it became necessary to do more than defend, the Danes were equal to the task. In one of the most successful escapes of World War II, they helped nearly all of their nation's Jews flee to the safety of neutral Sweden.

Germany and Denmark

In 1939, Denmark consisted of a few islands and a small slice of the European mainland. The population was less than 5 million. Although Denmark had once been a formidable military power, those days were long past by the time Hitler came to power. At the beginning of World War II, Denmark had few fortifications, few weapons, and an army consisting of only about fourteen thousand soldiers. That remained true in the first months of the war, too, even though the Danes feared that Hitler might try to launch an attack upon their country.

That lack of strong defense was intentional. Danish government leaders knew that they could never defeat Germany if Nazi officials decided to invade. They decided, therefore, to remain as neutral as possible and not to do anything that might offend their powerful neighbor. There might be a small advantage gained by building trenches to block the progress of German troops, or by increasing the size of the Danish army. But Danish officials reasoned that these small advantages would be more than lost if the Germans resented these moves.

The Danes' efforts, however, were in vain. In April 1940, the Germans claimed to have received word that the Allies were planning to invade parts of Scandinavia. To "protect" its northern neighbors, the German government de-manded control of both Norway and Denmark. Facing certain annihilation if they refused, Denmark's leaders immediately gave in. Within two hours or so after the initial demand, Denmark was firmly under the thumb of the Nazis.

The Quiet Occupation

The circumstances of the Nazi occupation, however, were unusual. Germany had taken most of the rest of its neighbors by force. German troops had destroyed homes in these countries and killed civilians and soldiers alike. In Denmark, on the other hand, the invasion was peaceful and subdued. Other than the arrival of new government officials and

Pictured is Copenhagen, Denmark, in the 1940s. Daily life for most Danes remained unchanged after Hitler occupied the country.

the presence of some scattered German soldiers, few Danes noticed much difference in their everyday routines.

There were two main reasons for the Nazis' relatively gentle treatment of the Danes. One was Denmark's quick capitulation: Hitler saw no reason to waste troops in taming an already tame country. The other involved Nazi racial theories. Culturally and ethnically, the Germans and the Scandinavians were closely related. Hitler believed in the genetic superiority of Germans and other Nordic peoples—a group that included the Danes. Thus, he was willing to tolerate the Danes while meeting other, less "desirable" ethnic groups with force.

Although occupied, Germany allowed Denmark to control most of its own affairs. The Nazis did not dissolve the Danish government or depose King Christian X. "Germany," the Nazis promised, "has no intention now or in the future of encroaching upon the Kingdom of Denmark's territorial integrity or political independence."[52] And for several years, the Nazis kept this promise. Despite the occupation, most decisions involving Danish concerns were made by the Danish government.

At first, not even Denmark's small Jewish population was affected by Nazi rule. In 1940, the country was home to only about eight thousand Jews, most living in the capital of Copenhagen. Perhaps because of the small numbers, the Danish Jews were well assimilated into Danish society. They were also respected by the Christians around them in a way that was extremely rare among European nations.

As a result, Danish citizens resisted Nazi views on Judaism. Nearly everywhere else in Europe, Jews were forced to wear yellow Stars of David to make them easy to identify, but in Denmark, they were not. Indeed, public officials went out of their way to protect and support the Jews. "I have heard with regret of the synagogue fire," wrote King Christian to Copenhagen Jews in 1942 after political vandals tried to burn their temple, "and am happy that the damage was slight."[53] Between 1940 and early 1943, the German government did not raise any objections to Danish support for the Jews, even as Nazis murdered and brutalized Jews in other countries across Europe.

Policy Changes

But as the war continued, the situation changed. The Nazis had expected to win a quick military victory over the Allied forces. By 1943, however, it was clear that the war would be longer, bloodier, and costlier than German officials had believed. Nor was there any guarantee that the Nazis would emerge victorious. Frustrated and angry, Nazi leaders were increasingly intolerant of those who did not agree with their policies. In particular, they began to question whether their permissiveness toward Denmark was really a good idea.

At the same time, public resentment of the Nazis was growing among the Danes. Even a relatively gentle occupation was still an occupation, and many Danes came to resist the German influence. "A strong feeling of hate began to

Jews wearing the Star of David as identification pose for a photo. Danish Jews were not forced to wear the stars.

build up in most people," said one Danish woman about the Danish reaction to the Nazis; "a desire to be allowed to do something to fight the enemy instead of just having to behave."[54] Acts of sabotage against the German army slowly increased, and the number of underground anti-Nazi newspapers grew accordingly.

By the summer of 1943, German officials began to clamp down on Danish dissent. Mild acts of protest that once had been tolerated were now grounds for imprisonment. One man was put in jail for a month for speaking to a German soldier in English. Nazi troops patrolled Danish towns and cities with weapons at the ready. And when some Danes declared a general strike in

protest of the new policies, a German general announced that those who struck would be put to death.

The Danish treatment of the Jews played an important role in the Nazi crackdown. As the Final Solution got underway elsewhere in Europe, Hitler became increasingly unwilling to leave Denmark's Jews alone. The very idea was loathsome, he told Werner Best, the head of the Nazi occupation in Denmark. And the notion that the Danes were not just tolerating but protecting the Jews especially galled the Nazis.

Despite the growing Nazi disapproval, the Danes were finding it more and more important to protect the Jews who shared their land. Part of the reason involved the long tradition of tolerance in Denmark. As early as 1690, the Danish government had rejected the idea of confining Jews to a ghetto as "an inhuman way of life,"[55] and religious freedom had been a cornerstone of Danish law since the early 1800s. With the occupation, however, protection of the Jews took on another meaning as well. By championing the rights of their fellow citizens, Danish gentiles were declaring their solidarity against the Nazi invaders.

"It Can't Happen Here"

By early 1943, the Jews of Denmark knew they were in a precarious position. Still, few went into hiding or tried to escape to a safer country. There was as yet no immediate threat to their lives and property, and Danish Jews were comfortable among their fellow Danish citizens. As one Danish Jew optimistically put it, "It can't happen here in good old Denmark."[56]

But as autumn approached, the Jews began to worry. Rumors flew that the Nazis would soon come to arrest them and deport them to concentration camps. If so, the Jews of Denmark intended to be ready. As one Jewish businessman recalled later on, "I felt it necessary to inform the personnel of my firm that we might have to leave the country." But without concrete evidence, the Jews remained cautious. "Personally," the businessman added, "I do not believe the rumors."[57]

Unfortunately, the rumors were true. In early September, Best had sent a chilling telegram to his superiors in Berlin.

"It is my opinion," he wrote, "that measures should now be taken toward a solution of the problem . . . of the [Danish] Jews."[58] He suggested transporting every Jewish man, woman, and child to the concentration camps. A few Nazi officials worried that such an action would cause tremendous public outcry in Denmark. But most liked the idea, and Best's suggestion was accepted.

Still, it was clear to all Nazi leaders that the Danes would react to the arrest of the Jews in ways other nationalities largely had not. They expected resistance from locals in their search for Jews. Nazi officials thus decided to act swiftly and secretly. On October 1 and 2, they resolved, they would quietly round up all Danish Jews and send them to the camps. There would be no prior announcement. The operation was to come as a complete surprise.

In spite of the rumors swirling through Denmark, the Nazis thought they had an excellent chance of completing the raid. The tales of mass arrests were vague and insubstantial. They gave no dates; they did not specify who would carry out the raid and how the Jews would be deported. Moreover, the Nazis had promised Danish leaders that they had no such plans, and their assurance convinced at least some influential Danes. As September came to an end, the Nazis thought they had managed to quell the rumors.

"We Must All Be in Hiding"

They were mistaken. In order to carry out the proposed raids, Nazi leaders in

Germany needed to alert German police officers and other officials stationed in Denmark. Among the people they informed was a German national named Georg Duckwitz. A resident of Denmark for the past fifteen years, Duckwitz had strong Nazi leanings; indeed, he ran Danish shipping operations for the Nazis. But despite his close connections to the German government, he did not hate the Danish Jews. In late September, when Duckwitz learned of the raid, he was furious. "I know what I have to do,"[59] he wrote in his diary.

On September 28, Duckwitz began to spread word of the upcoming raid among Jews and Danish leaders. At first, most were reluctant to believe him. In fact, when the president of Copenhagen's Jewish community heard the news from one of Duckwitz's friends, he flatly replied, "You're lying."[60] Still, Duckwitz had a good reputation in Denmark, and his work for the German government put him in a position to know the Nazis' intentions. Most Jews decided they could not afford to disregard the warning completely.

During the next two days Jews and their Danish supporters hurried to alert everyone they could find of the proposed arrests. Jørgen Knudsen, a gentile ambulance driver involved in the resistance, seized a phone book, called everyone he could find who had a Jewish name, and warned them to leave their homes. Another Danish Christian burst into the office of his doctor, a Jew, and demanded to see him right away. "Is it an emergency?" the doctor asked impatiently. "Yes," the Dane replied, "it's very definitely an emergency."[61]

The messengers were helped in their effort by the Jewish religious calendar: September 30 marked the beginning of Rosh Hashanah, the Jewish New Year. To celebrate the holiday, many Jews gathered for worship that afternoon in the Copenhagen synagogue. But Rabbi Marcus Melchior canceled the service. Telling the members of his shocked congregation about the raid, he urged them to protect themselves. "By nightfall tonight," he said, "we must all be in hiding."[62]

"You Don't Even Know My Name"

In the two or three days before the anticipated raid, Jews slowly and quietly left their homes for the safety of churches, hospitals, and the houses of friends and neighbors. Most had no trouble finding a place of refuge. Some Jews showed up on a gentile friend's doorstep unannounced, explained the situation, and were taken in for a night or two. Others had friends who contacted them first, offering a spare room, a basement, or a summer cottage for as long as necessary.

Danes offered shelter to complete strangers, too. Among those who escaped arrest in this manner was a Jewish factory foreman named Mendel Katlev. Hearing word of the invasion while he was at work, Katlev boarded a train for home. He had no close gentile friends and feared for his family's safety. The

Jewish resistance fighters pose with their weapons. Many Danes were willing to protect Jews from the Nazi raid.

train's conductor, noticing that Katlev seemed pale and shaken, asked him casually what the trouble was. When Katlev told him the story, the conductor leaned closer. "Come to my house," he urged. "Get your wife and children and bring them all to my house." "But you don't know me," Katlev pointed out, startled. "You don't even know my name."[63]

It did not matter. Katlev was one of many Danish Jews who took refuge that day with people they barely knew. The Danes knew they could be arrested for shielding their Jewish neighbors, but most were willing to take the risk. "We must obey God before we obey man,"[64] announced the Lutheran bish-op of Copenhagen, urging the Danes to protect as many Jews as possible. Throughout Denmark, hundreds of Danes did exactly that.

Failure of the Raid

The raid, when it came, was a terrifying experience for the people of Denmark, but particularly so for the Jews. The Nazis cut all telephone wires late on October 1. German police officers, accompanied by a few pro-Nazi Danes, surrounded houses and smashed in doors of apartment buildings. Sometimes they left if no one answered the ring of the doorbell; more often, they woke up the neighbors to ask if anyone had seen missing Jewish families. "The most frightful scenes were played out," recalled one Danish writer, "with whole families being dragged away."[65]

Thanks to Duckwitz's warning and to the speed at which ordinary Jews and Danes sounded the alarm, however, Nazi troopers mostly found empty houses on the night of October 1. A few Jews had refused to believe the warnings, and a few others were too old or sick to move easily. These men, women, and children, perhaps two hundred in all, were captured and immediately deported to concentration camps in eastern Europe.

The rest, though, were safe. They had evaded the Nazis, at least temporarily. "A living wall," writes one historian, "[had been] raised by the Danish people in the space of one night."[66] Of all Nazi operations directed against the Jews during and before the war, the "living wall" had made this one by far the least successful.

More Danger

Unfortunately, the Jews of Denmark could not stay concealed forever. Reports were circulating throughout Denmark that the escape had infuriated Hitler and his officials. It seemed clear that the Nazis would soon start searching through gentile homes and offices to root out the remaining Jews.

Nazi guards march a family of Jews out of the Warsaw ghetto in Poland. Most Danish Jews avoided the 1943 Nazi raid by hiding.

Neutrality and Sweden

In 1943, Sweden was one of a handful of officially neutral countries in Europe. A small nation far to the north of most of the fighting, it had few resources and little military value. Thus, both sides were content to leave it more or less alone.

But if Sweden was neutral in theory, it was not necessarily so in practice. At the start of the war, in particular, the Swedish government worked from time to time with the Nazis. It made some sense: Germany was the closest superpower, and the Swedes were anxious not to offend Hitler. Moreover, many Swedes expected that the Germans would soon win the war. They thought it would be wise to be on their side when that happened.

By the summer of 1943, though, the situation had changed. If anything, the Allies now held the upper hand. Moreover, the brutality and viciousness of Nazism was increasingly clear. While the Swedes were not willing to give up their neutrality, they were now more prepared to assist the Allies. This shift away from Germany helped make it possible for the Swedish government to accept the Danish refugees over Nazi objections. Had the crisis occurred a year or two earlier, it is much less likely that Sweden would have participated.

In the days following the operation, Nazi soldiers rounded up over two hundred more Jews who had not concealed themselves well enough or who came out of hiding too soon. It seemed clear that the rest would soon be captured, too, if they stayed where they were.

There was one chance of permanent escape, though—to head for Sweden, a neutral country just a few miles across open water from eastern Denmark. A handful of Jews and other dissidents had already left Denmark for Swedish territory soon after the arrival of the Nazis. Despite the short distance, however, getting to Sweden was not easy. German ships patrolled the sound that divided the two countries, hidden mines threatened to blow up boats that attempted the trip, and stiff penalties awaited those who tried to smuggle passengers across to Sweden.

There seemed to be little choice, however. Working closely with resistance workers and other Danish supporters, leaders of the Jewish community soon came up with a daring plan: All of Denmark's Jews would escape to Sweden. Once again, ordinary citizens roamed the cities and villages of Denmark in order to spread the news. This time, though, their task was much harder. Not only were tensions high, but the Jews were scattered and no longer easy to find.

But through sheer persistence, word soon reached nearly all the country's Jews. Beginning just after the raid, thousands of Jews left their hiding places and set off for Elsinore, Gilleleje, and other seaside towns of eastern Denmark. Some traveled by train, others by taxi or by private car. When they could, they took back roads and roundabout routes in order to evade suspicion. However they traveled, their eventual goal was the same: to cross the strait to the safety of Sweden.

The Jews knew that they were taking a terrible risk. Had they known what was going on, the Nazis could easily have stopped this mass exodus. In fact, Nazi patrols did capture a number of Jews as they made their way to the seashore. On the evening of October 4, for instance, a group of Jews arrived at the town of Dragør, where they were met by a bus full of German soldiers. Although some of the Jews escaped into the night, at least a dozen were caught and sent to a concentration camp.

Most of the Jews, however, made it safely to the coastline. Some observers believed that the Nazis were completely unprepared for the suddenness with which the country's Jews headed for the sea. "It all happened so fast," reported an eyewitness. "[The Nazis] were taken by surprise and fooled."[67] Danes on the country's police forces also generally ignored the Nazi directive commanding them to search for Jews.

Across the Strait

Getting the Jews to the seashore was only half the battle. It was still necessary to transport them across the strait to Sweden—a distance of anywhere from five to thirty miles, depending on the starting point. The Nazi warships and explosives off the coast made this a difficult task. So did the fact that the Germans had confiscated most large ships from the Danes. All that remained were small rowboats, sailboats, and wooden fishing vessels. These were slow and not designed for large groups of passengers, but they would have to do.

Earlier in the war, the people of the fishing villages had been unwilling to risk their freedom to help dissidents escape. After hearing about the raids, though, they had changed their minds. Townspeople gladly concealed the runaways in their churches, schools, and homes until they could get safe passage to Sweden. Likewise, most of the fishermen were now willing to ferry people across the water. Some, to be sure, charged enormous fees. But they were balanced by those who accepted only token payments—or refused to take any money at all.

At first the escapes were disorganized and random. Individual Jews approached individual captains and made arrangements for transport. But as October continued, the escapes became more carefully planned. One Danish man bought a boat expressly to bring runaways to the Swedish coast. Jews and gentiles joined forces to set up safe passage routes to the coast or negotiated with fishermen on behalf of dozens, even hundreds, of refugees at once.

Still, the dangers of escape were great. Despite the help of the Danish police, those who crossed the water were indeed risking their lives and their freedom. Secrecy was critical. The slightest sound

Friends help a Danish Jew from his hiding place on a boat that successfully transported him to Sweden.

could alert the Nazis to the presence of a ship in the area. Passengers were cautioned to remain absolutely silent as they boarded the boats. Speaking was expressly forbidden until the boat had crossed into Swedish waters—and sometimes not even then.

Young children posed a particularly acute problem, as it was essential that they be silent aboard the boats. On the earliest trips, some passengers threatened to drown or suffocate children who cried out. "Throw him overboard!"[68] insisted a man when Bent Bogratschew's little brother could not keep quiet. Bogratschew's mother, fortunately, had come prepared; she quickly gave the boy a sedative to make him

sleep. Thereafter, young children were routinely drugged before the voyage began to keep them quiet.

"Like Herrings in a Barrel"

The circumstances of the escapes differed from one night to another. Generally, they began with Jews concealing themselves by the sea and waiting for a signal to board a nearby boat. "[We] were herded into the hold [the storage area at the bottom of a boat]," remembered one anonymous escaper, "like herrings in a barrel."[69] If there were too many passengers for the hold, they would be wrapped in fishing nets and bags and told to lie still on the deck.

Before picking up the passengers, the ships had already been prepared to host their human cargo. Captains had doused the lights and wrapped oars in cloth to muffle the noise they made. They had usually dusted the decks, too, with a concoction made from cocaine and dried human blood. The reason for this involved German police dogs, which sometimes sniffed out people on the small fishing boats. A Danish scientist had discovered that the mixture deadened the dogs' sense of smell and made it impossible for them to detect humans.

What happened after loading the boats depended on the weather, the presence of patrols, and the seaworthiness of the vessel. In some cases, the refugees arrived safely in Sweden after a quick dash across the sound. More commonly, though, the boats moved slowly and cautiously. They had to avoid mines and patrols, and often they battled heavy rains, high winds, and choppy seas as well. Maneuvering at night was difficult even for experienced captains, let alone for the novices who sometimes piloted the boats. Several vessels lost power partway across the strait. Others sprang leaks. Some boats took up to twenty-four hours to reach Sweden.

To the escapers packed tightly aboard the boats, the crossings were agonizing. Even if the trip went smoothly,

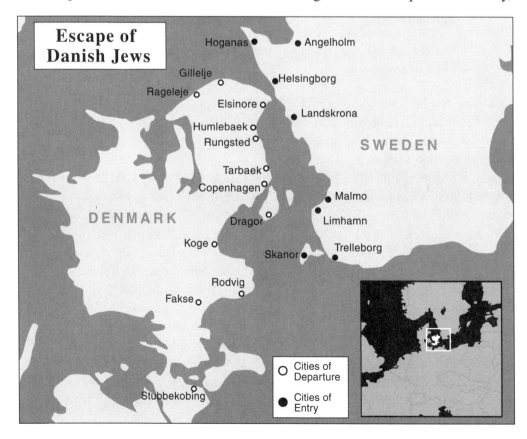

Escape of Danish Jews

Hoganas •   • Angelholm

Gillelje ○   • Helsingborg
Rageleje ○
    Elsinore ○
      • Landskrona
Humlebaek ○
Rungsted ○

    SWEDEN

Tarbaek ○
Copenhagen ○
    • Malmo
DENMARK   Dragor ○   Limhamn
Koge ○
    Skanor •   Trelleborg

Rodvig ○
Fakse ○

○ Cities of Departure

• Cities of Entry

Stubbekobing ○

The Cost of Escape

The escape from Denmark was extremely expensive. By one estimate, Jews and their supporters spent over six hundred thousand dollars to rent fishing boats, pay captains, subsidize transportation costs for those too poor to pay the fees, and bribe German officials not to turn them in. But Denmark's Jews were determined to escape, and they were equally determined to share resources as much as possible in order to leave no one behind. Jews sold possessions and borrowed whatever they could from friends and business associates. Underground groups helped immeasurably as well.

So did perfect strangers. After arriving safely in a seaside village, for instance, one man was crushed to discover that he could not afford passage to Sweden for himself and his family. Learning of his plight, a Danish woman who lived nearby offered to help. Later in the day, she obtained the necessary money from a Lutheran pastor. "Though it was ostensibly a loan," the man's son recalled later, quoted in Michael Berenbaum's book *The World Must Know*, "the pastor refused repayment after the war."

the refugees found themselves fearing the worst. Each light was surely a German patrol; each new wave threatened to rip the boat apart. "Every muscle was tense for fear of discovery,"[70] wrote one passenger. For some, these fears came true. A few boats hit mines, came apart, or lost their way. Others were intercepted by German patrols. About thirty refugees drowned while on their way to Sweden. A few dozen more were arrested after leaving the harbor. And a small number of Danish Jews, unable to manage the stress of the escape, committed suicide.

Although these Jews did not reach the safety of Sweden, more than seven thousand others did. By the end of the fall, astonishingly, about nine of every ten Danish Jews had successfully crossed the straits. No other occupied European country could boast such a survival rate.

Once in Sweden, the Jews of Denmark were truly safe. Sweden retained its neutrality throughout the rest of the war. It was one of the few European countries never disturbed by the Nazis.

The escape operation had included nearly a thousand trips across the sound. It had required massive coordination among thousands of organizers and refugees. It had taken courage and perseverance, both from those who escaped and from those who assisted the refugees. But most of all, it had relied on cooperation between the Jews of Denmark and the Danish gentiles. "Virtually all our countrymen reacted against this meaningless injustice and brutality," one Danish Jew wrote with pride after the war. In the days before and during the escape, the writer added, "the staunch solidarity of all Danes found its most brilliant expression."[71]

5

Attack at Sobibor

NOT ALL ESCAPES from Nazi persecution were carried out with secrecy and stealth. In a few cases, escapes were the result of mass uprisings in places where Nazi security was unusually tight: most often, concentration camps and the Jewish ghettos of eastern Europe. These uprisings were intended to overpower Nazi guards and make escape possible. Brandishing whatever weapons they could find and catching their captors by surprise, these prisoners hoped to inflict damage on the Nazis and make their way to safety before the Nazis could respond.

Nearly all of these attacks were doomed. The superior arms of the guards beat back most revolts before prisoners could escape. But a few revolts were quite successful, at least in

the short term. Through careful planning and precise execution, the people involved in these actions managed to kill some of their Nazi tormentors and make a permanent escape. Among the most successful of these revolts took place in 1943 at the Sobibor concentration camp in eastern Poland.

Sobibor

Built in 1942, Sobibor was relatively small compared to other Nazi concentration camps. For most of its existence, the entire facility covered a space of only about six-hundred-by-four-hundred yards. Its small size hinted at its purpose. Sobibor had no need for extra space to house its inmates. Instead, it functioned as one of the Nazis' most lethal death camps.

Being sent to Sobibor was, quite literally, a death sentence. The camp had been built to kill as many Jews as possible. The compound contained three gas chambers, each of which accommodated about two hundred people; the chambers were in steady use from the time the camp opened to the time it closed in late 1943. New prisoners arrived almost daily by train. Nearly all went immediately to the gas chambers. By the middle of 1943, the Nazis of Sobibor were murdering several thousand prisoners a day.

Most transports, however, included a handful of people who were not immediately put to death. They were instead assigned to fill work crews around the camp. Some of these prisoners were skilled laborers—shoemakers, carpenters, and so on. Others were strong enough to handle heavy lifting. At any given time there were perhaps six hundred men and women on work detail. These Jews were not told what was happening to the others, but they could usually guess what was going on. There was no other explanation for the steady disappearance of those who arrived each day.

Escape Attempts

During the first year of Sobibor's operation, several work crew inmates attempted to escape from the camp. Prisoners tried to cut through the barbed wire that surrounded the compound. They dug tunnels that they hoped would lead them to freedom. They even tried to bribe the guards to

Prisoners push carts of rocks at the Plaszow concentration camp in Poland. Those who were strong enough to work at Sobibor were not put to death upon arrival.

look the other way while they ran into the nearby forests. But the results of most of these attempts were the same. In nearly every case, the men and women who tried to escape were quickly recaptured or killed in the process.

The Nazis responded to each escape attempt by making escape even more difficult than it already was. As in Auschwitz, guards randomly shot and killed dozens of prisoners each time there was an escape attempt. The guards also shored up their disciplinary procedures, eventually requiring three roll calls a day to make sure no one could go missing for long. And they strengthened their defenses outside the camp's boundaries as well, adding a minefield and a ditch full of water.

Still, the prisoners in Sobibor did not give up their hope and desire for freedom. An organized underground movement dedicated to resistance soon sprang up among the inmates assigned to work details at the camp. Despite the close supervision and the long work hours, these prisoners managed to plan and discuss possible escapes among themselves. By early 1943, the members of this underground movement had come up with several potential plans for mass escapes.

However, none of these suggestions seemed likely to succeed. Even the best of the plans seemed unrealistic. One proposal, for instance, involved setting a camp building on fire in hopes that prisoners could run away as the guards busied themselves extinguishing the blaze. Another plot called for prison cooks to poison the food of the Nazi officials who ran the camp. As the summer of 1943 ended, members of the underground at Sobibor had tried only a handful of these plans, but none had proved effective.

A New Arrival

On September 23, 1943, a new train arrived in Sobibor. This transport, from the city of Minsk, in present-day Belarus, included some Russian prisoners of war as well as Jews. Among the eighty or so passengers chosen for work detail was a Soviet army officer named Alexander Pechersky. In addition to fighting for the Soviet Union against Germany, Pechersky was a Jew; thus, he was doubly an enemy of the Nazi Party. Captured early in the war, Pechersky had been held in various Nazi prison camps for nearly two years.

Unlike some of the earlier arrivals to Sobibor, Pechersky discovered the true purpose of the death camp almost from the beginning. Noticing columns of smoke rising in the distance, the new prisoner casually asked a Jewish worker, Leon Feldhendler, what was going on. "Your comrades' bodies are burning there," Feldhendler told him, "the ones who arrived together with you." Shocked and appalled, Pechersky pressed for details. Feldhendler quietly described the process by which the arrivals were murdered. "We will also burn," Feldhendler explained in closing; "if not tomorrow, then in a week or a month from now."[72]

The news was grim, but Pechersky had great emotional strength. Two years in Nazi prison camps had not destroyed

A trainload of prisoners rolls in to a concentration camp. When Alexander Pechersky arrived at Sobibor he was determined to resist the Nazis.

his spirit. He had even attempted an escape from a Belarussian prison a year earlier. Besides, Pechersky was not alone at Sobibor. Many of the other Russian inmates on the work detail had served with him in the army or had been imprisoned with him at other camps. Already, these men looked to him as a leader.

Moreover, Pechersky reasoned, he had nothing to lose if he refused to give in to the situation. According to Feldhendler, all Sobibor prisoners were going to be put to death sooner or later. Thus, it made sense for Pechersky to take any opportunity to resist the Nazis, no matter the risks. If he failed, he would probably be killed; but then, death would be his fate even if he did nothing at all. For Pechersky, the only chance of survival lay in challenging the Nazis—and in finding a way out of Sobibor.

"A Clap of Spring Thunder"

Pechersky lost no time in establishing himself as a leader of the Sobibor prison workers. On his first day of work, he and his fellow Russians were commanded to sing Russian songs for the entertainment of the camp's Nazi officials. Thinking quickly, Pechersky suggested to his fellow prisoners that they sing a song called "If War Comes Tomorrow."

The Russians were dismayed. "If War Comes Tomorrow" was a song of the anti-Nazi resistance movement in Russia. They feared that the Nazis would recognize the Soviet patriotism in the song and would respond with anger. "Are you crazy?" one of Pechersky's fellow officers snapped. "They'll shoot us."[73] But Pechersky paid no attention. He began the song; and before long, the others joined in.

As Pechersky guessed, the Germans did not understand the words. They had no idea that the Russians were singing a song expressing anti-Nazi sentiments. But some of the other prisoners, especially those from the nations of eastern Europe, understood Russian and knew right away what was happening. Even those who spoke no Russian quickly caught on: In their choice of music, these new arrivals from the Soviet Union were refusing to give in to the Nazis.

The episode boosted Pechersky's profile among the other members of the work crews. "The soldier had spunk,"[74] Feldhendler told himself with admiration. Just as important, the act of singing a resistance song gave the prisoners much-needed hope. Perhaps it was possible, after all, to maintain self-respect, even in a terrible place like Sobibor. "In this camp of death and despair," Pechersky wrote afterwards, "the Soviet song rang out like a clap of spring thunder."[75]

Mass Resistance

Within a few days, Pechersky had earned the full respect of his fellow prisoners. Other inmates began seeking his advice and opinions, particularly about the question of escape. Pechersky counseled others to be patient and to plan any escape attempts as thoroughly as possible. "With what will you cross the wire fence?" he asked a group of Russians who were considering a hasty dash for the woods. "And how will you cross the mine field?"[76] When the Russians realized they had no answers to these questions, they postponed their attempt.

In Pechersky's view it was unacceptable for the prisoners of Sobibor to try to escape singly or in small groups. For an ordinary prisoner-of-war camp, Pechersky thought, such a strategy might work. But in a camp like Sobibor, where escape attempts were met with extreme brutality, individual escape attempts seemed not only foolhardy, they seemed unethical as well. "What about the others?" Pechersky asked another prisoner who had proposed that the two of them try to hack through the fence. "When we go, we'll all go together. The whole camp."[77]

As he got to know his surroundings, Pechersky became more and more convinced that the only chance of survival lay in mass resistance. Somehow the entire corps of workers would have to band together and stage a revolt against the armed guards. Such a revolt would need time for planning, and once again Pechersky suggested patience. A hasty and disorganized attack, he knew, could never succeed.

Unfortunately, time was not on the workers' side. Each day, more Jews arrived at the camp, bound for the gas chambers. Each day, the workers labored to the point of exhaustion and sometimes beyond. Winter was approaching, bringing snow that would make escapers' tracks easy to follow. Besides, there were rumors that the camp might soon be closing. It seemed likely that the workers would be murdered as soon as the camp was no longer in use.

Despite the problems, the mood among the workers was now more cheerful than it had been before the arrival of the Russians. Pechersky and his fellow soldiers brought with them energy and military know-how. For the first time, members of the work crew held out hope that there might actually be a way out. "We had thought about [escape] more than once," Feldhendler told Pechersky, "but we didn't know how. . . . We trust you. Act."[78]

A Plan of Escape

Over the next two or three weeks, Pechersky spent his time asking questions of his fellow inmates. Anything he could learn about the operations of the camp might help him in planning an escape. Some of the prisoners, for instance, knew where the explosives were buried in the minefield outside the compound. Pechersky found out what time the guards changed shifts; he learned where the camp officials stored their weapons; he learned whatever he could about the layout of the camp.

By early October, Pechersky had devised a possible plan of escape. Aware that the work camp might contain informers, though, he confided in very few fellow prisoners. Feldhendler knew some of the details. So did Shlomo Leitman and Alexander Shubayev, Jews

Luka

One of the minor characters in the story of the Sobibor escape was a young woman known to us today only as Luka. A German Jew and the daughter of a Communist, she was about eighteen at the time of the uprising. Pechersky noticed her soon after arriving in the camp. "Her whole being exuded confidence," he wrote years later, as quoted in Yuri Suhl's *They Fought Back*. Seeking her out, he spent as much free time around her as possible.

Pechersky's purpose was not romantic. Although he came to admire and respect Luka's intelligence and courage, he was actually using the young woman as a decoy. When they saw Pechersky spending his time with a pretty woman, the guards assumed this was a matter of a young man pursuing a romantic interest in a woman; consequently, they took little notice of him.

That was a mistake. Pechersky's conversations with Luka were frequently interrupted with asides to other leaders of the resistance—all of them in Russian, a language Luka did not speak.

Luka knew little of what Pechersky was planning. In part from a sense of chivalry, but mainly because he was unsure that he could trust her to keep silent, Pechersky chose not to confide his plans in her until the revolt was already underway. Years later, he would wish things had been different. "I regret to this day that I didn't trust her," he told an American reporter, as quoted in Richard Rashke's *Escape from Sobibor*. "That I didn't tell her [in advance] about the escape."

Luka's fate is unknown. She made it to the forest as part of the escape, but she probably did not survive the war.

American soldiers somberly look over a pyre of burned bodies at a concentration camp in Germany. Sobibor used such pyres for its victims as well.

who had arrived on the same transport as Pechersky. And on October 12, Pechersky called a meeting of other leaders of the resistance to tell them what was going on. Still, even then, the bulk of Sobibor's workers knew little or nothing about Pechersky's intentions.

Pechersky, did, however, share information with two rather unlikely people. The Nazis often staffed concentration camps with so-called *kapos*—inmates who were given special privileges in exchange for helping to oversee and discipline the workers. Usually the other inmates despised the *kapos*, and for good reason: Some served as informers, and most seemed to take delight in tormenting their fellow prisoners. Thus, Pechersky at first took great pains to keep information away from the *kapos*.

But he soon changed his mind. The *kapos*, he realized, could be of enormous help in a revolt. They carried small arms and were given freedom of movement unavailable to the other inmates. Besides, the *kapos* of Sobibor did not trust the Nazis. Despite their privileges, they knew that their own situation was precarious at best. "When the time comes to liquidate the camp," one *kapo* admitted to Pechersky, "they'll kill us too."[79] Seeing their potential value, Pechersky brought two of the *kapos* into his confidence.

Revolt

Pechersky's plan was bold but simple. It consisted of two parts. First, the prisoners would lure as many German officers as possible into the workshops where the skilled workers labored.

There, inmates would kill the officers with hatchets made secretly by the prison blacksmith. Once the Germans were dead, the prisoners would storm Sobibor's gates and fences, their hatchets supplemented by the officers' pistols. Pechersky knew that many would die in rifle fire from the Ukranian guards. But if all went well, perhaps some would make it to the safety of the woods.

Pechersky and the other leaders chose October 14 as the day for action. The prisoners divided the hatchets among themselves, along with a few razor blades and knives they had taken from the workshops. Pechersky's friend Shlomo Leitman chose the men who would carry out the killings, and Pechersky himself determined each one's assignment. "It has to be done in such a way that [the victim] shouldn't utter a sound,"[80] he reminded the assassins. Silence and secrecy were essential. If even one German officer should escape to alert the rest, the plot would be doomed.

At four that afternoon, the deputy commander of the camp, Josef Niemann, arrived at the tailor shop. The *kapos* had told Niemann that a new uniform was ready and that he needed to come in for a proper fitting. But the tailor was not the only prisoner in the workshop. The moment Niemann came inside, Pechersky's old comrade Shubayev stole out of a hiding place and smashed his hatchet into the commander's head, killing him.

The prisoners' first victim was dead. There would be more to come, some of them scheduled for execution in the same tailor shop where Niemann had died. Shubayev took Niemann's pistol and hid the body beneath a bunk in a nearby storeroom. He and the tailor cleaned up the bloodstains so as not to arouse suspicion. Then Shubayev returned to his hiding place and awaited his next victim.

"For All the Jews"

The exact sequence of events that afternoon will never be known. Accounts differ widely as to where and in what order the German officers were killed. What *is* clear is that the first part of the plan was highly successful. During the next hour, the leaders of the resistance killed one German officer after another, all without any of the guards noticing. One Nazi was killed in the shoemaker's shop while trying on a new pair of boots. Others were waylaid in a warehouse as they awaited a chance to try on a new leather jacket. Several more were dispatched while guarding another part of the camp.

Despite the dangers and the gruesome nature of their task, few of the assassins had second thoughts. "I was happy for the opportunity given to me to kill a German,"[81] remembered one prisoner, and his reaction was typical. For months, even years, the inmates had been brutalized by their Nazi tormentors. Their livelihoods had been taken away and their homes destroyed; nearly all had lost family members through Nazi atrocities. Now, finally, the prisoners had a chance for revenge. In their zeal for vengeance, a few could not keep quiet. "For my father!" shouted an inmate as he thrust his weapon into the skull of another officer. "For my brother! For all the Jews!"[82]

But there was more to do than kill. Feldhendler cut the telephone wires leading from the administration building, preventing the Nazis from easily summoning reinforcements. Another prisoner shut down the power supply. Pechersky hurried to tell the rest of the inmates what was going on and to ready them for the second stage of the plan. He had little patience with those prisoners who professed fear or anxiety.

Tunnel to Freedom

Before finalizing the escape plan the prisoners would ultimately use, Pechersky toyed with the notion of digging a tunnel to freedom. He told a few trusted friends how the plot would work, down to the length, depth, and circumference the tunnel would need to be in order to be effective. He even worked out where the prisoners could hide some of the dirt moved during the digging and calculated that the escape would have to begin at eleven o'clock at night.

But as Pechersky told it later, the tunnel idea was never more than an alternate plan in case the uprising should prove impossible to carry out. Creating a tunnel, he decided, simply involved too many drawbacks. He was unsure whether the tunnel could be dug to specifications, or indeed at all; it would have had to stretch from the barracks to the woods at least thirty-five yards distant. Moreover, the longer the tunnel grew, the more likely it would be that guards or fellow inmates would notice the work.

And finally, Pechersky did not trust the prisoners to calmly take their turns in line. The process of moving six hundred inmates through the tunnel would be, at best, agonizingly slow. He worried that fights would break out as prisoners grew impatient. That was especially true because there was no way of knowing whether all the inmates could successfully crawl through before the alarm was raised. In the end, a few prisoners did some preliminary digging, but the tunnel idea was soon abandoned.

Pechersky abandoned his initial plan to escape from Sobibor by digging a tunnel.

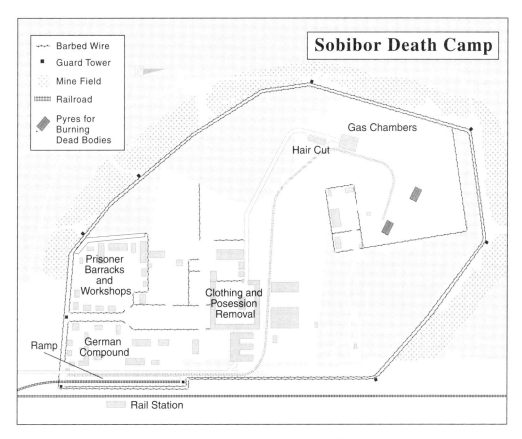

Sobibor Death Camp

Legend:
- Barbed Wire
- Guard Tower
- Mine Field
- Railroad
- Pyres for Burning Dead Bodies

Gas Chambers

Hair Cut

Prisoner Barracks and Workshops

Clothing and Posession Removal

Ramp

German Compound

Rail Station

"What we are doing now is the only way to stay alive," he told a young woman who questioned the plot. "You understand? We must live."[83]

By five o'clock, only one of the highest-ranking German officers remained alive. Alone among his fellow Nazi commanders, Karl Frenzel had skipped his appointment in the workshops. "The scoundrel did not come," lamented the man chosen to kill Frenzel. "Until today I am sorry for that."[84] Pechersky debated whether to send a squadron in search of Frenzel, but ultimately decided not to take the time. Escape was more important, in the end, than revenge.

To the Fences

At a little after five, the bugle sounded to gather the inmates for the afternoon roll call. Unknown to the guards, though, the bugle had a second meaning to the six hundred or so prisoners of the work crews. As Pechersky and the other leaders of the revolt had just told them, it was the signal to prepare for the mass escape. The goal was to gather quietly and wait until the roll was halfway done before breaking for the outside.

But tensions were too high. The prisoners were a jittery mass of emotions. It seemed impossible for any of the inmates to stay in line. Seeing that the prisoners could no longer be controlled,

Pechersky decided to give the order to charge. "Our day has come," he cried out as the group neared the main gate. "Most of the Germans are dead. Let's die with honor!"[85]

Pechersky's words did the trick. "United Jews from Russia, Poland, Holland, France, Czechoslovakia, and Germany," Pechersky wrote later, "six hundred pain-racked, tormented people, surged forward with a wild 'hurrah' to life and freedom."[86] Most headed directly for the main gate of the camp. Several dozen inmates, though, made for the armory, hoping to cut off the guards from their source of weapons. The attackers did not succeed in taking over the armory, but the group nevertheless managed to make off with several rifles.

By now, however, the guards posted elsewhere in the camp were on high alert. They rained fire on the prisoners from the camp's watchtowers and from the ground, concentrating especially on the space just in front of the camp's main entrance. Frantically, the prisoners ran back and forth, searching for an escape route. All semblance of order was lost, and Pechersky gave up hope of an organized assault on the gate. "Riot and confusion prevailed," remembered inmate Ada Lichtman. "Everything was thundering around."[87]

As Pechersky had anticipated, many of the prisoners died as they attempted to escape. Some inmates were shot as they ran forward, machine-gunned to death by the guards. Others became tangled on the barbed wire that surrounded the camp. Still others lost their footing or became disoriented in the chaos. And a few, certain they would be shot if they tried to escape, could only remain where they were. Almost none of these unfortunate prisoners survived.

But there were too many inmates for the Nazis to catch them all. And there was too much at stake for the leaders of the escape to give in. As the Nazi shooting intensified, the resistance leaders returned fire with their stolen weapons. They killed the only guard standing at the main gate and at least two more in the watchtowers. By now, though, their purpose was not so much to take more lives as to cover the escape of the other prisoners. In this, the shooters were successful.

With the main gate suddenly unguarded, some of the prisoners dashed out the entrance. A few fell, hit by gunfire, but many more made their way through the gates without being hit. Other prisoners, armed with hatchets, scissors, and wire cutters, cut open the barbed wire and hurried into the fields beyond. And a few climbed over the fence, using a ladder that a worker had hidden the previous evening. Astonishingly, more than four hundred of the six hundred prisoners managed to make it past the fences.

The Mines

There remained one more obstacle before the prisoners could conceal themselves in the forests. That was the minefield recently installed beyond the gates of Sobibor. Pechersky's original plan had called for the prisoners to throw rocks and planks into the fields before crossing them. The idea was to explode as many mines as possible before anyone entered the area. But with gunfire echoing behind them, the panicked inmates did not have time for this. Nor could most recall the locations of the mines. Instead, they plunged headlong into the fields.

For the first wave of those who tried to cross the fields, the results were tragic. The Nazis had planted the explosives so that nearby footsteps would trigger

Aftermath

The prisoners were not fully free once they had reached the woods beyond Sobibor. Cold, tired, and hungry, the escapees were still deep inside Nazi-occupied territory. They knew they soon would be the subject of a massive manhunt. Nor could they expect help from the local population. Not only would Nazi officials do their best to intimidate nearby Poles who might be of service to the runaways, but the Polish population at the time was largely biased against Jews—even those who had escaped from the Nazis.

To make matters worse, there was no obvious place for most of them to go. Most came from Jewish ghettos and small towns now razed or cordoned off by the Nazis. Few had families and friends to return to. And the ones who did would have to travel many miles across unfamiliar territory in order to reach their former homes. For most of the escapees, therefore, the best chance of survival lay in reaching one of several small groups of anti-Nazi partisans, freedom fighters who took refuge in the forests and did their best to sabotage Nazi plans. Indeed, Pechersky's plan was for the escapees to divide into small groups once they reached the woods and try to find the partisans. But the odds of doing so were long.

In fact, most of the escapees did not survive the war. Some died of hunger or of wounds received as they fled. About one hundred were recaptured by Nazi patrols summoned in the wake of the uprising. A few, seeking emergency help, knocked late at night on the wrong doors and were turned in by local Nazi sympathizers. Others, like Pechersky's friend Alexander Subayev, joined partisan units, but were killed as they fought the Nazis. Others, like Pechersky, fought and survived. Perhaps fifty of the prisoners lived through the war, perhaps more; no one knows for sure.

Survival after the escape was indeed an ordeal. "We were murdered not only by Germans," wrote escapee Dov Freiberg, quoted in Yitzhak Arad's book *Belzec, Sobibor, Treblinka: The Operation Reinhard Death Camps*, "but by Poles, Ukrainians, and [anti-Jewish] partisans. . . . More than once we considered suicide, after we saw that the whole world was against us." But there were a few good people in Poland and the Ukraine, Freiberg noted, people who helped the runaways at great risk to themselves. And Freiberg never regretted the escape. As he put it years afterwards, "I would not have exchanged the whole terrible period in the forests for one day, even the best day, in Sobibor."

Survivors of the Sobibor uprising pose for a photograph in 1944. They are among the estimated fifty prisoners who ultimately survived through World War II.

them, and one by one the bombs went off as men and women streamed toward the forests. "A mine exploded nearby," recalled Ada Lichtman. "I could see a body being lifted into the air and then falling down."[88] Perhaps 150 of those who escaped through the fences died in the explosions on the minefields.

But the Nazis had never anticipated a mass escape of the Sobibor inmates, so there were not enough mines to stop the progress of all the fleeing prisoners. After the carnage of the first few minutes, nearly all the explosives were spent. That allowed free passage toward the woods for the prisoners at the rear. By unwittingly exploding the mines, those who died had helped those behind them to live.

As for those who successfully navigated the mines, the safety of the forest was now at hand. "And there we were," recalled Pechersky, "on the other side of the mine field! Already we had run a hundred yards! . . . And running faster, faster, through the barren strip of land, bodies so nakedly exposed to the eyes of the pursuers, so unprotected from bullets! Faster, faster, and into the woods, among the trees, under cover. And there I was—in their shadow."[89]

For the moment, at least, Pechersky was safe. And so were many others.

Freedom

Within a few minutes, Sobibor was quiet once more. The death toll among the prisoners had been huge. An estimated two hundred of the six hundred prisoners lay dead or mortally wounded in and around the camp. Another one hundred or so, unable or unwilling to try to break through the camp's defenses, hid themselves in out-of-the-way corners of the compound; nearly all would be found and executed within the next day or so. Of the six hundred inmates who marched to the roll call that October day, half would never reach the other side of the minefield. And many of those who did would not survive the war.

Still, the escape from Sobibor had been a tremendous success. About three hundred inmates reached the relative safety of the woods that afternoon. Through careful planning and great courage, they had successfully broken through the defenses of one of the most diabolical of all Nazi concentration camps. Under terrible circumstances, Pechersky and the other prisoners had carried off a seemingly impossible task. They had fought back. And they had won.

Appendix

Documents Pertaining to the Holocaust

Seeking Refuge

This document is taken from the account of a German Jew who emigrated to the United States after Adolf Hitler came to power. This man—known to us today only by his first name, Rudolf—owned a farm in southern Germany. A veteran of World War I, he considered himself as much German as Jewish. Indeed, he was unwilling to emigrate even after the Nazis arrested him and sent him to a prison camp in Sachsenhausen, Germany. Soon after his release in 1933, though, the farmer changed his mind—and began the arduous process of finding a way to escape the country.

My wife had been trying to arrange that I should emigrate at once to Cuba alone. I said no—"I'll stay here on the farm even if they beat me dead." I knew of no dishonest thing I had done in my life, and I knew I had done my duty by my country.

I was supposed to report to the police station every day, but the mayor exempted me. Some days later, though, I was ordered to come before the "*Ortsbauernführer*" [a local official], and he said to me—although he owed me money himself:

"Rudolf, your farm has been made into an 'Erbhof' (a farm to be owned only by Aryans)—so you must sell it."

I said, "I'll think about it."

After a while an officer came up to my place and told me again that I would have to sell. I said to him:

"Who built this house—you or I?"

In my own house we almost came to blows, and he left saying that he'd put me back where I'd been [that is, the prison camp Sachenhausen].

So I decided to leave.

The date set for my emigration was September 6th. I went to several different consulates for a visa, but I had no luck. I knew there was a chance in America, and tried to get on the refugee lists for the United States, but there was not enough time. Then I got a visa to Panama because I was a farmer. But my sister who lived in America sent me a newspaper clipping that said the central refugee committee was looking for a farmer to settle in a community in the U. S. A., if he already had his affidavit [a sponsorship from an American] and a number—the number of registration at the consulate. I could get an affidavit from my sister, and I was registered at the consulate, but my number was so high that it seemed I'd have to wait for two years.

In the meantime the date set for my emigration in September had come. The local police warned me to leave, and let me get out with my family although they had a warrant for my arrest in their pockets already. When we were gone our house was broken into right away, and all our good things smashed, and the windows broken.

We took our auto and for sixteen days and nights we travelled—just anywhere. We didn't know where to go. It seemed safest to stay every night in a different place. So we always kept moving—sixteen days and sixteen nights.

One day the news reached me that I was supposed to report to Berlin. I was scared to go there, so I managed to get a postponement by telephone. I was in touch with our mayor all this time by telephone and he advised me to stay away for a while still—he'd tell me when it was safe to come home. But for me it seemed impossible to keep up that life. I finally went to a police station in a large city, reported myself with my wife, and told them my case. They gave me a letter releasing me from arrest. We went back to the farm.

I had to make the trip to Berlin to get my admission to America—to see if they would accept me as one of the farmers to be settled there. I was selected from a big group of applicants, and they even gave me a special letter to hasten the granting of the American visa in [the city of] Stuttgart. But the consul in Stuttgart wanted a lot of papers and complicated proofs. It took a long time, until I got a French transit visa—a four weeks' stay in France—that would make it possible for me to get out of Germany. They granted the transit visa on the old Panama visa I'd received some months before.

Alone, I set out for Strasbourg [a city in France]. My wife stayed behind to get our things together, pack them, and send them on.

The children were also with her. In Strasbourg the American consul told me to go to Paris for my American visa. There the refugee committee supported me while I had to wait, and put me in a hotel. My wife sent our two children on to me under care of a friend, but I had no place to keep them, so I had to put the girl in an orphan asylum and the boy stayed with a French family.

That was an awful time for me. I didn't have much to eat, and there was much waiting at the consulates. At last I got my wife admitted.

In the meantime our boy had had an accident. One day he burned himself very badly. He had to be rushed to the hospital and was in danger of death. That was the same day that I was to go and get my visa, which had been granted at last. I got to the offices ten minutes late, and so couldn't get it any more. They told me that I'd have to start all over again.

This was when my wife arrived. It was towards the end of August, 1939. She'd had a terrible time at home. She had tried to get as many of our possessions together to take with her as possible, since you couldn't take money out. During that time great areas in our district were being evacuated for military purposes, and they wanted to put these evacuated people on the Jewish farms. Luckily for us, there was a dispute among our local officials, and because of that we were able to have the sale of our farm delayed, so my wife got a little time to get ready. But she had to buy many new things, because most of our old ones had been broken when they raided our house.

When at last she was ready to go, they said she couldn't emigrate as long as the farm was still in our name. So she had to go through the business of the sale, although she couldn't take the money from it with her!

From William Allan Neilson, ed., *We Escaped: Twelve Personal Narratives of the Flight to America.* New York: Macmillan, 1941.

A New Identity

Many Jewish children escaped Nazi persecution by taking refuge with gentile families. Some remained hidden for weeks or even years, living in an attic or a small out-of-the-way spare room. Others were hidden in plain sight—brought to church, sent to religious schools, and passed off as Christians. This excerpt comes from the recollections of Nicole David, a young Jewish girl from Profondeville, Belgium, who spent some of the Nazi years living with a Christian family.

At the café Daddy ordered an aperitif [an alcoholic drink]. He let me have a sip of it, which made me feel grown-up. I can picture the scene before us: the lovely river and the rocks of Lustin on the opposite bank looked so peaceful that I completely forgot about the Gestapo [the secret state police]. Then we started walking home. As we approached our corner, we could see three German trucks right outside our house. Suddenly I wanted to run home, to see if my mother was all right. Then a man I'd never seen before intercepted us and warned us not to go home. I started to cry: I was frantic to see my mother. Daddy said, 'Be quiet. The Gestapo might hear you.' That was when I first learned not to cry, a lesson that stayed with me for years and years.

The man, who was from the Resistance, took us down a narrow road to a 'safe' house, where an Italian woman took us to her attic. We stayed there for the rest of the day. Daddy told me not to go near the window. Members of the SS and soldiers in German uniform passed back and forth all day while they looked for us.

That evening a non-Jewish friend of my mother's came and tried to reassure me that my mother was all right. She said that my mother had sent a message that I shouldn't worry because my father would look after me. At that moment I got terrible, terrible stomach cramps, but I wasn't allowed to go down to the toilet. Instead a pot was brought up for me. Later that night . . . a woman came to take me to the family of Mr. and Mrs. Gaston Champagne, Château Saint Servais, Saint Servais, Namur. It was very dark on the way, and I was terribly afraid.

I found myself living in a large Catholic family with ten children, though only five were still at home. The youngest was sixteen. I didn't know these people! In fact it was through one of the adult sons just two days earlier that my mother had made the arrangements for me. Life seemed strange there. I couldn't go to school. The only regular outing was to church with the family. Most of the time I was by myself and quite lonely. Each day I spent hours and hours making up fantasy stories, the kind my father used to tell me. They always involved Mickey, an imaginary friend, and he could do everything. I had not been a loner by nature. I loved company and loved to talk. But I developed into a very self-sufficient person.

The house, which looked like a castle, was surrounded by a very large garden. A high wall went all around it, and I could not see the street, except through the gate, which they told me to stay away from. I do not remember any flowers in the garden. There was a small, empty pond, with concrete sides I liked to slide down. Doing that tore my panties, which annoyed Madame Champagne, but it was the only game I had.

This family was good: they willingly risked their lives, and they never took any money for keeping me. One of the daughters used to say to me, 'Don't forget your Jewish prayers.' Still, it didn't feel like home. I had been a much loved, pampered, and rather willful child. One time, for example, I had eaten thirty sugar cubes. My mother had hidden them, but I'd stood on a chair and then a shelf to get them anyway. That's how I was! However, in the hiding family there were strict rules. The children addressed their parents as *vous* instead of the informal *tu* [French forms of the word "you"] generally used, and I had never heard such formality in a family. In this thirty-nine-room house that seemed more like a museum, with the large paintings and heavy furniture, we had to be given permission to join the grown-ups in the salon (living room).

I had to learn to do without the hugs and all the special treatment I was used to. For example, my father had always tucked me in with bedtime stories. Now I had to go up two flights alone in the dark in this enormous house. That was torture for me! The windows were covered with black cloth because of the blackout. Everything creaked. Sometimes the two teenage boys in the family would play jokes on me, making strange noises at the top of the stairs. As a result for years afterward I was terrified of the dark. In fact it's only in the last five or six years that I can tolerate it, even in my own house!

I had been a picky eater at home, and my mother used to run after me with healthy food. She'd lovingly fed me spinach (along with stories of Popeye), fish, and porridge. But the minute I came to the family Champagne, I sat down and ate with everyone else—even though the food was unappealing. It was strictly what we could have on the ration books: mostly boiled potatoes and boiled red cabbage. The bread was so bad that before eating it one had to break the piece in half to see if it formed threads, which meant it could not be eaten. What was hardest for me was having to sit quietly until the meal was finished.

I was told I had picked up bad manners . . . so I had to learn to eat my soup without slurping. I learned fast! It wasn't that I feared my rescuers would turn me out, but I understood the need to be a good child and not make trouble. In fact one day I went to mass with a terrible toothache. That, to me, was 'being good.' Later they noticed my swollen cheek and took me to a friend who was a dentist.

During this time I rarely thought of my mother. I understood that she was gone, and the only way I could cope or make sense of life at that point was to detach myself and just do whatever was required at the time. My father came to visit once. He was hidden at the bottom of a small van, dressed in workman's clothes. I was overjoyed that we got to spend a night together. (That night I had somebody to go up in the dark with me!) When he left in the van the next morning, the Champagnes warned him not to come again because it was too dangerous.

From Jane Marks, *The Hidden Children*. New York: Fawcett Columbine, 1993.

Escape from the Ghetto

Like many other eastern European towns under Nazi occupation, the community of Lachwa, Belarus, had a Jewish ghetto, or area where all the local Jews were required to live. In Lachwa, the ghetto consisted of two small streets, which were home to nearly two thousand Jews. The Nazis intended to kill all two thousand, but in August 1942, the inhabitants of the ghetto staged a revolt. In the confusion, several hundred of Lachwa's Jews were able to escape. Some of them made it successfully to freedom. The names in the account are mainly those of ghetto residents.

When several members of the ghetto committee, the Judenrat, approached the Germans and asked why they had come here, they replied calmly that they came to liquidate the Jews of the Lachwa Ghetto and added, "But we decided to let thirty of you live, including the members of the Committee and about three to four people of every useful trade. . . . And now 'be so kind' and ask the gathering to go back home and wait there until we call for them. . . ."

At this, Dov Lopatin, president of the ghetto committee, cried out, "You will not murder us piecemeal! Either we all live, or we all die!"

At this moment the SS men [the Nazi paramilitary force] entered the ghetto and ordered everyone to line up. Instead, the Jews ran to their houses and set them on fire. Dov Lopatin was the first to apply the torch to the headquarters of the Judenrat. Soon all the others followed his example. Smoke and flames shot up in the air. A panic arose among the SS. They fired into the crowd. The first victims fell. They were Abraham Slutzki and Israel Drepski.

Yitzchok Rochtchin attacked the SS chief with an ax. The SS officer fell to the ground, covered with blood. Having no way out Rochtchin jumped into the nearby river. He was struck down by a bullet. At the same time another SS man was felled at the gate by Chaim Cheiffetz and the brothers Asher and Moshe-Leib Cheiffetz. Still another German fell at the hands of Moshe Klopnitzki.

Now the crowd was aroused and stormed the ghetto gate. Those who were able to run did, leaving behind a flaming ghetto. They were pursued and shot at. Many fell. The town was littered with corpses. People ran with their last ounce of strength to the forests near the river Pripet, hoping to find a haven there. Of the 2,000 Jews, about 600 managed to reach their destination. But the police . . . murdered most of them brutally. The forester Polin with his own hands shot about 200 Jews.

The Germans succeeded in leading to the grave only a few, because young and old alike ran. They would rather die from a bullet while running than be led to the grave.

Several days later 120 Lachwa Jews gathered in the Chobot forest, about twenty kilometers from town, and joined the partisans, fighting side by side with them, and later with the Red Army, thus taking revenge for their beloved ones.

From Yuri Suhl, *They Fought Back*. New York: Schocken Books, 1975.

Escape from German Aggression

Mitzi Abeles was a Yugoslavian Jew who was forced to flee from advancing Nazi soldiers on multiple occasions. In late 1942, after several narrow escapes, Abeles traveled to a village near Zagreb, Yugoslavia, where she received help from several local residents. It would be more than a year before Abeles would be truly safe.

[Near Zagreb] a peasant woman hid and maintained me under the condition, to be sure, that I stay at all times in the attic. Only at night was I allowed to come down to relieve myself and gather up food for another day. The attic was very cold and I developed bad rheumatism there. The police entered the house several times during searches and I escaped them narrowly. Once I had time only to cover my hair with a rag and to throw myself under the bedcovers. The agents were already coming up the stairs and the peasant woman declared with false calm that I was her sick mother. On another occasion I climbed out of the window and hid behind the smokestack until the agents were gone. In my poor condition I felt these experiences as physical strain and nervous tension. In February 1943 the peasant woman gave me to understand that I could no longer remain with her. Sick as I was, I therefore moved to one of her acquaintances in *Sestinski Dol.* He was a railway employee whose route was *Zagreb-Spalato* and in July 1943 he enabled me to get to Spalato. This city, the former Yugoslav Split, [that is, once a part of Yugoslavia, when the city was known as Split] was now under Italian rule and the Jews there were relatively safe. . . .

I remained in Spalato until September 10, 1943. From there I fled by boat to the island of Lagosta. During my stay in Spalato, on September 2, 1943, the Italians had capitulated [surrendered] to the Allies. Since Italy was now joining the Allies, the Germans occupied most of Italy and marched into Dalmatia [a region near the Italian-Yugoslavian border]. Spalato was bombed heavily. I lived there with relatives who had a small baby. During the bombing I held the infant in my arms. The apartment was hit by a bomb and the mother (with whom I was related) died under it. The father of the child was missing afterward; his body could not be found. The child and I were not scratched. I succeeded in sending the baby to Zagreb to his Christian grandparents. The names of my relatives were *Zdenka* and *Zwonko Kollman*.

After this tragedy, the Germans moved into the city. On that day I stood helplessly on the beach not knowing where to turn. Suddenly I saw a small fishing vessel crowded with a group of people. One of the persons on board motioned me to join them. It turned out to be an acquaintance of mine. Just at the moment when German troops were entering the city he offered me the opportunity to cross to the island of Lagosta which was reported to be still unoccupied by the Germans.

The trip was torture. We spent four days in this nutshell at sea. Since we had neither food nor water, older people lost consciousness in the sun. At Lagosta some of the men went into the village. They found a military radio transmission station which the Italians had abandoned. One of the men, who was a professional operator of such equipment, reported to Bari [an Italian city] that the island was unoccupied and that we were a small refugee group from Spalato who were trying to get to Bari. We stayed on Lagosta for 14 days. Then on a moonless night we crossed, constantly afraid of German aircraft. When we reached Bari, we encountered the Jewish Brigade from Palestine. They took us to their messhall and I recuperated in their camp. We were all completely unkempt, and physically as well as psychologically in poor condition.

From Raul Hilberg, ed., *Documents of Destruction.* Chicago: Quadrangle Books, 1971.

Escape Through Enemy Territory

Richard Glazar was a Jew from Czechoslovakia. As a young adult, he was imprisoned in Treblinka, a concentration camp in Poland. In August 1943, Glazar and some of his fellow prisoners escaped from the camp as part of an uprising. Despite their escape, Glazar and his friend Karl were by no means yet free. Instead, they found themselves in unfriendly territory and had to use all their resources to avoid being recaptured. This excerpt begins soon after their escape.

As the sun begins to set, but still in daylight, we leave our hideout in order to orient ourselves before it gets too dark. An endlessly wide plain spreads out before us. On the horizon beyond, we can see a weighted wooden beam rising into the sky, and we assume that it must be part of a well tower. The little house next to it seems to be alone on this flat piece of the world. It lures us like a vision, even though we know it may also mean danger. Will we ever reach it? We have been running from one stand of bushes to another for so long, and the well-water gallows is still so far off in the distance. But when the little house finally begins to grow larger, we can see signs of life. A woman in a head scarf, her back bent, is approaching the well.

We have to try, we have to ask, but from a distance. We don't know who else might be in the hut. Even the old woman might be dangerous. Anyone we meet may be an enemy. Her face turned toward us, the old woman stops, but she doesn't really seem all that surprised to see us. "Well, going to Warsaw, to the Vistula [River]? This Is Ostrów. You should be going the other way, over there. It'd be best just to keep following the road." She stands up a little straighter and looks us over more carefully: "*Uciekacie z niewoly, tak?*—You're escaping prisoners of war, aren't you? But you're not Poles . . ."

"*Tak, tak*—yes, yes," we nod. "My Czechy—from prison camp, we're Czechs. . . "

We disappear into the twilight behind the next stand of bushes and repeat the magic formula that the old woman unwittingly set on our tongues. "Hey, now do you know who we are and what we're doing? We're Czechs, and we're escaping from a prisoner of war camp. She must have seen lots of prisoners of war passing by here. Poles, maybe a Russian or two, a Ukrainian. Why not a few Czechs too? Yes, we're Czechs, and we want to get back home, somewhere off to the southwest."

First past Warsaw and over the Vistula. We can both remember at least that much of our geography lessons. But we're complete failures when it comes to navigating by the stars. Our Boy Scout skills have left us in the lurch, but not our luck—not yet, anyway. Up to this point we have actually been heading toward the Russian front. And this is probably our great good fortune, since the Germans will hardly have thought of sending a search party off in this direction. What a marvelous blunder.

Things that seem simple by twilight, when you can easily see the road to Warsaw leading off between rows of trees, become difficult by night. From time to time we even have to walk along the shoulder of the road in order not to lose our way. In complete darkness we bump into each other, and we practically have our noses in the signs before we can spell out the names of towns and villages—Wyszków, Radzymin. How many nights have we been walking since we escaped Treblinka? We don't know anymore. We begin to see signs of a more densely populated area: beams of light that cut through the darkness, fences, and barking dogs.

On one of these nights a command rings out from the direction of the road: "Halt!" We run away and hide in a potato field, lying motionless for hours. It looks as if we'll have to give up walking so close to the road, since there are houses everywhere. We're going to have to risk traveling by daylight, at least for a while, so that we can avoid settlements. It's okay. We even have the feeling that this has become less dangerous than moving at night. Each day we leave our hiding place a little earlier. Grazing cows, like guideposts, let us know which direction we should be taking. From the other side we are protected by long rows of bushes that are supposedly here to keep the wind from scalping the low-growing vegetation off these flat fields.

By the light of day we can seek out an isolated hut and wait for the appropriate time to ask for a little something to eat. The magic formula "We are Czechs, escaping prisoners of war," continues to work. And in these situations it is better to speak only Czech. It seems strange, but because it is a Slavic language we can make ourselves understood.

"Don't worry. Now, during the war years, we see so many people passing through—Poles, Russians, and whoever else. Our feelings tell us to feed a hungry man and ask no questions. Your good sense tells you to eat your fill and then continue on your way." These are the words a peasant woman used to reassure us.

One day we are following a path that intersects so abruptly with a small village lane that we cannot avoid a group of people walking our way. Among them are two German soldiers in uniform. Nothing happens. We walk right past them, and no one pays us any attention. Of course, by now we look exactly like the ragged speculators of the region—both of us barefoot, one of us with dry muddy boots slung over his shoulder, our pants torn practically to shreds. It is impossible to tell what color our crumpled shirts and jackets once were. With a new sense of self-assurance, we simply walk along the sidewalks past houses big and small, continuing on our way. From road signs we read the names of places we have never heard of before—Rembertów, Solejuwky.

From Richard Glazar, *Trap with a Green Fence.* Translated by Roslyn Theobald. Evanston, IL: Northwestern University Press, 1992.

Judith Strick Escapes

Nazi brutality continued even as World War II was coming to an end. Although Germany was nearly defeated, Nazi officials decided to move prisoners to other camps that might be deeper in German-held territory. In March 1945 Judith Strick and her fellow concentration camp inmates were marched out of one such prison when Allied forces came near. Strick and several of her friends decided to try to escape during the march. Franz, referred to several times in the text, was a Nazi storm trooper assigned to help bring Strick and the others to the new camp. When he became drunk one afternoon, Strick decided the time for escape had come.

We'd escape tonight because it would be more difficult later. Franz would sleep a drunkard's sleep. I would talk to Zellermayer, our sentry. I hoped he wouldn't stop us. The SS women were quite inoffensive. They were just young girls from Austria who longed to be home with their parents.

I walked over to Zellermayer. "And what will happen if we want to escape? What will you do, Zellermayer?"

"What *should* I do? I don't know. I am just as miserable as you. I don't know what has happened to my wife."

"Zellermayer, you won't shoot? Or if you must, then don't aim directly at us. Just over our heads in the air."

"I will shoot. It is my duty. I would be executed if I didn't. But I won't aim at anybody, I assure you."

I thanked him in the name of the girls.

We must escape tonight.

Franz went to sleep with one of the SS women and abandoned us to the care of the guards. The other guard didn't hear too well and had a stiff neck. He slept most of the time.

I had no fear that Zellermayer would aim at us. He could not aim in the dark even if he wanted to. We lay down but soon got up. There were perhaps ten or eleven of us. None of the others had moved.

Then we began to run. We heard Zellermayer's shots, but they were wide of the mark. We ran wildly. I saw a fenced-off church. We ran into the yard. I lost the girls behind me. I climbed over the fence, jumped over the graves. Then I came to another fence. It was covered with barbed wire. I scratched myself, but I climbed over it. Then I hid myself in a wood on a mountain side.

After I had got back my breath, I tore off my striped garments and stood in a blue sweater and long pants. I climbed the mountain and rested on the other side. Then I heard someone calling, "Where are you?" It was Tamara.

"Yes, here I am," I cried.

No one was pursuing us.

"What do you think, Lydia? What shall we do now?"

"I think we should retrace our steps. We'll head north till we reach the front."

We came to a stream and drank for a long time. We walked for a long time through the woods. We passed empty houses. There was no one around. No dogs barked at us, and in the houses there were no signs of life. We wanted to rest, but it was too dangerous. I didn't know whether they were looking for us, and we were still not far from the camp. We kept going till sunrise. Then we decided to sleep. We slept and slept and slept. I didn't dream at all but just slept quietly, my first sleep in freedom.

From Judith Strick Dribben, *A Girl Called Judith Strick.* New York: Cowles Book Company, 1970.

An American Airman Flees

Ernest de los Santos was an American gunner whose plane was shot down by the Nazis in 1943. He made three escape attempts from a prisoner-of-war camp known as Stalag 7-A. Although he was recaptured each time, de los Santos showed creativity and daring; his experience is a reminder that successful escape was extremely difficult.

I escaped from Stalag 7-A at Moosberg three times. The first time I was by myself. I watched the way the guards were spaced.

About ten feet away from the main fence was a wire and beyond that was the death area. They would shoot you without question if you were caught in this no-man's-land. That night I stripped down to my shorts and rolled my shirt and trousers real tight and carried them over my shoulder with a strap I had made. I sneaked out of the barracks and crawled out to the warning area and watched how the tower light worked. Then I made a dash for it. There were double fences, about ten feet apart with a lot of barbed-wire entanglements. I went over the first fence with no trouble and jumped down. I started for the next fence, but my shoe string got tangled up in the barbed wire, and I couldn't get it loose. The guards had tied tin cans to the fence, and when I pulled on my shoe lace, the wire rattled. When this guard came over to see what the noise was, he found me. He was supposed to shoot me, but he started yelling instead. I guess he was just so proud he had caught someone trying to escape. The tower guard put his light on me and asked the guard why he hadn't shot me. He couldn't because his gun was not loaded. When I heard him put a shell in the chamber, I looked right at him and thought, "Well, this is it." I just stood there staring at him. The tower guard kept yelling at him to shoot, but he didn't. He let me crawl back over the fence and took me to the officer in charge who put me in solitary confinement.

Some of the camps had escape committees [that is, groups who planned to escape together], and that was all well and good, but someone planning to escape was not going to talk to anybody. A lot of us who escaped were loners, and a loner keeps things to himself. After I had escaped the second time and got caught, somebody—I suppose it was the escape committee— set up a meeting for all escapees to talk among themselves and to compare notes. They said maybe this would help those planning future escapes. Several of us went, but a funny thing happened. Each of us sat by himself, getting as far away from everybody else as he could. We weren't about to sit next to anybody, and we weren't planning on talking to anyone either.

I just had to try and break out. The other prisoners wouldn't even try. I don't know why. If you don't try, you'll never do it. I just wasn't going to sit in the barracks. I didn't really have any friends, so I'd go out for a walk and start looking around to see how I could get out—and I'd find a way. Each day I'd think about it a little more, and then I'd decide to take a chance. You knew you were going to get caught, but you just chose to go anyway. If you are determined, there's a way out. You just have to see your chance and take it. Evidently, nobody else was trying to escape because after I made it out the third time, the escape committee wondered how I did it. I told them, once you make up your mind, nobody's going to hold you.

The second time I escaped I went with a buddy. He stuck right on my coat tail. He wasn't about to let me out of his sight. I couldn't shake him, and we got caught the first night out. The next time he went with me again. Red Cross parcels had arrived on a fourwheel wagon, and I sneaked under it. There was a metal band hanging below the wagon bed, and I was able to crawl up and rest on it. Several of the prisoners saw me do it, including my buddy who decided he had to tag along. So here he comes. He crawled up and laid on top of the back axle. We stayed there from about three o'clock in the afternoon until dark when they came for the wagon. The guard at the front gate waved us out, and we had two or three nights of very cold, rainy weather. We human beings can't stay out in the weather too long. My buddy talked me into walking in the daylight. If I had been by myself, I would have holed up in the daytime and walked at night. But he insisted we walk in the daylight. We were heading for Switzerland. The first day we got away with it. The soldiers didn't pay any attention to us. But kids and women were suspicious as hell. The second day they turned us in. A constable came after us with a gun and took us back to Moosberg.

From Lewis H. Carlson, *We Were Each Other's Prisoners.*
New York: BasicBooks, 1997.

Notes

Introduction: Hitler and the Nazis

1. Quoted in Michael Berenbaum, *The World Must Know*. Boston: Little, Brown, 1993, p. 21.
2. Quoted in Martin Gilbert, *Auschwitz and the Allies*. New York: Holt, Rinehart and Winston, 1981, p. 20.

Chapter One: East from Lithuania

3. Quoted in Hillel Levine, *In Search of Sugihara*. New York: Free Press, 1996, p. 143.
4. Zev Birger, *No Time for Patience*. New York: Newmarket Press, 1999, p. 18.
5. Quoted in Alison Leslie Gold, *A Special Fate*. New York: Scholastic, 2000, p. xi.
6. Quoted in V. Stanley Vardys, ed., *Lithuania Under the Soviets*. New York: Praeger, 1965, p. 54.
7. Quoted in Birger, *No Time for Patience*, p. 31.
8. Quoted in Berenbaum, *The World Must Know*, p. 50.
9. Birger, *No Time for Patience*, p. 38.
10. Quoted in Levine, *In Search of Sugihara*, p. 232.

11. Quoted in Levine, *In Search of Sugihara*, p. 235.
12. Quoted in Levine, *In Search of Sugihara*, p. 234.
13. Quoted in Mordecai Paldiel, *The Path of the Righteous*. Hoboken, NJ: KTAV, 1993, pp. 253–54.
14. Quoted in Levine, *In Search of Sugihara*, p. 252.
15. Quoted in Paldiel, *The Path of the Righteous*, p. 254.
16. Quoted in William Zinsser, ed., *Going on Faith*. New York: Marlowe, 1999, p. 77.
17. Quoted in Levine, *In Search of Sugihara*, p. 247.
18. Quoted in Zinsser, *Going on Faith*, p. 78.
19. Quoted in Paldiel, *The Path of the Righteous*, p. 255.
20. Quoted in Zinsser, *Going on Faith*, p. 81.

Chapter Two: Escape from Auschwitz

21. Quoted in Terrence Des Pres, *The Survivor*. New York: Oxford University Press, 1976, p. 35.

22. Quoted in Walter Laqueur, *The Terrible Secret*. Boston: Little, Brown, 1980, p. 146.
23. Wieslaw Kielar, *Anus Mundi*. New York: Times Books, 1972, p. 3.
24. Filip Müller, *Eyewitness Auschwitz*. New York: Stein and Day, 1979, p. 61.
25. Quoted in Berenbaum, *The World Must Know*, p. 131.
26. Müller, *Eyewitness Auschwitz*, p. 80.
27. Quoted in David S. Wyman, *The Abandonment of the Jews*. New York: Pantheon, 1994, p. 335.
28. Quoted in Deborah Dwork and Robert Jan van Pelt, *Auschwitz, 1270 to the Present*. New York: W.W. Norton, 1996, p. 175.
29. Quoted in Claude Lanzmann, *Shoah: An Oral History of the Holocaust*. New York: Pantheon, 1985, p. 165.
30. Quoted in Gilbert, *Auschwitz and the Allies*, p. 193.
31. Müller, *Eyewitness Auschwitz*, p. 121.
32. Quoted in Yuri Suhl, ed., *They Fought Back*. New York: Schocken Books, 1967, p. 206.
33. Quoted in Suhl, *They Fought Back*, p. 205.
34. Quoted in Gilbert, *Auschwitz and the Allies*, p. 196.
35. Quoted in Gilbert, *Auschwitz and the Allies*, p. 202.

Chapter Three: Escape from Colditz

36. P.R. Reid, *The Colditz Story*. Philadelphia: Lippincott, 1953, p. 12.
37. Quoted in Henry Chancellor, *Colditz*. New York: HarperCollins, 2001, p. 10.
38. Quoted in Chancellor, *Colditz*, p. 11.
39. Reid, *The Colditz Story*, p. 13.
40. Reid, *The Colditz Story*, p. 157.
41. Aidan Crawley, *Escape from Germany*. London: Her Majesty's Stationery Office, 1985, p. 44.
42. Quoted in Chancellor, *Colditz*, p. 156.
43. Reid, *The Colditz Story*, p. 240.
44. Reid, *The Colditz Story*, p. 254.
45. Quoted in Chancellor, *Colditz*, p. 184.
46. Reid, *The Colditz Story*, p. 263.
47. Quoted in Roger Howard, *Great Escapes and Rescues: An Encyclopedia*. Santa Barbara, CA: ABC-CLIO, 1999, p. 62.
48. Reid, *The Colditz Story*, p. 266.
49. Quoted in Chancellor, *Colditz*, p. 187.
50. Reid, *The Colditz Story*, p. 281.
51. Quoted in Chancellor, *Colditz*, p. 187.

Chapter Four: Out of Denmark

52. Quoted in Leni Yahil, *The Rescue of Danish Jewry*. Philadelphia: Jewish Publication Society of America, 1969, p. 32.
53. Quoted in Yahil, *The Rescue of Danish Jewry*, p. 63.
54. Quoted in Harold Flender, *Rescue in Denmark*. New York: Manor Books, 1964, p. 33.
55. Quoted in Flender, *Rescue in Denmark*, p. 28.
56. Quoted in Yahil, *The Rescue of Danish Jewry*, p. 216.

57. Quoted in Yahil, *The Rescue of Danish Jewry*, pp. 180–181.

58. Quoted in Ellen Levine, *Darkness over Denmark*. New York: Holiday House, 1999, pp. 64–65.

59. Quoted in Levine, *Darkness over Denmark*, p. 68.

60. Quoted in Flender, *Rescue in Denmark*, p. 44.

61. Quoted in Flender, *Rescue in Denmark*, p. 49.

62. Quoted in Flender, *Rescue in Denmark*, p. 16.

63. Quoted in Flender, *Rescue in Denmark*, p. 53.

64. Quoted in Berenbaum, *The World Must Know*, p. 158.

65. Quoted in Yahil, *The Rescue of Danish Jewry*, p. 184.

66. Yahil, *The Rescue of Danish Jewry*, p. 188.

67. Quoted in Flender, *Rescue in Denmark*, p. 69.

68. Quoted in Levine, *Darkness over Denmark*, p. 82.

69. Quoted in Yahil, *The Rescue of Danish Jewry*, p. 259.

70. Quoted in Yahil, *The Rescue of Danish Jewry*, p. 260.

71. Quoted in Yahil, *The Rescue of Danish Jewry*, p. 381.

Chapter Five: Attack at Sobibor

72. Quoted in Suhl, *They Fought Back*, pp. 11–12.

73. Quoted in Richard Rashke, *Escape from Sobibor*. Boston: Houghton Mifflin, 1982, p. 159.

74. Quoted in Rashke, *Escape from Sobibor*, p. 159.

75. Quoted in Suhl, *They Fought Back*, p. 14.

76. Quoted in Suhl, *They Fought Back*, p. 21.

77. Quoted in Rashke, *Escape from Sobibor*, p. 167.

78. Quoted in Yitzhak Arad, *Belzec, Sobibor, Treblinka: The Operation Reinhard Death Camps*. Bloomington: Indiana University Press, 1987, p. 309.

79. Quoted in Suhl, *They Fought Back*, p. 29.

80. Quoted in Suhl, *They Fought Back*, p. 34.

81. Quoted in Arad, *Belzec, Sobibor, Treblinka*, p. 327.

82. Quoted in Rashke, *Escape from Sobibor*, p. 225.

83. Quoted in Suhl, *They Fought Back*, p. 37.

84. Quoted in Arad, *Belzec, Sobibor, Treblinka*, p. 328.

85. Quoted in Rashke, *Escape from Sobibor*, p. 229.

86. Quoted in Suhl, *They Fought Back*, p. 39.

87. Quoted in Arad, *Belzec, Sobibor, Treblinka*, p. 331.

88. Quoted in Arad, *Belzec, Sobibor, Treblinka*, p. 331.

89. Quoted in Suhl, *They Fought Back*, p. 40.

For Further Reading

Books

Livia E. Bitton-Jackson, *I Have Lived a Thousand Years*. New York: Simon and Schuster, 1997. The recollections of a woman who survived Nazi oppression.

David K. Fremon, *The Holocaust Heroes*. Springfield, NJ: Enslow, 1998. The stories of the people who helped save as many Jews as possible during and before World War II.

Alison Leslie Gold, *A Special Fate*. New York: Scholastic, 2000. A readable biography of Chiune Sugihara, with special emphasis on his help in the escape of the Lithuanian refugees.

Clive A. Lawton, *Auschwitz*. Cambridge, MA: Candlewick Press, 2002. About the Auschwitz concentration camp and its inmates.

Ellen Levine, *Darkness over Denmark*. New York: Holiday House, 1999. Well-illustrated description of the Danish Jews' escape, together with a discussion of the Danish resistance movement. Levine based her account largely on the memories of Danes and Danish Jews who lived through the period.

Milton Meltzer, *Rescue: The Story of How Gentiles Saved Jews in the Holocaust*. New York: Harper and Row, 1988. Descriptions of moments during World War II in which non-Jews helped shelter and protect Jews. Includes useful background information as well as a discussion of the flight of the Jews from Denmark.

Websites

Holocaust Educational Resource (www.nizkor.org). A thorough look at the Holocaust and the Nazi years. Includes a wealth of information on Nazi persecution.

Remember.org (www.remember.org). A large site filled with valuable information about Nazi terror and its effects on the people of Europe.

The Simon Wiesenthal Center (http://motlc.wiesenthal.com). Information and resources on World War II and the Holocaust. Includes many primary sources.

The United States Holocaust Memorial Museum (www.ushmm.org). The website of a Washington museum dedicated to studies of the Holocaust.

Works Consulted

Books

Yitzhak Arad, *Belzec, Sobibor, Treblinka: The Operation Reinhard Death Camps*. Bloomington: Indiana University Press, 1987. Includes important information on the escape from Sobibor. Also gives valuable background on Sobibor and two other nearby death camps.

Michael Berenbaum, *The World Must Know*. Boston: Little, Brown, 1993. A comprehensive history of the Holocaust; profusely illustrated with photos of people, places, and artifacts.

Zev Birger, *No Time for Patience*. New York: Newmarket Press, 1999. Birger was a Jew born in Lithuania. He survived the Holocaust, but most of his family did not. This is his memoir.

Henry Chancellor, *Colditz*. New York: HarperCollins, 2001. A description of the many escapes carried out by the prisoners of war in the Colditz prison.

Aidan Crawley, *Escape from Germany*. London: Her Majesty's Stationery Office, 1985. Escapes of British pilots from German prisons during World War II. The author himself broke out of a prisoner of war camp in 1942 but was recaptured before reaching home.

Lucy S. Dawidowicz, *From That Place and Time*. New York: W.W. Norton, 1989. An American Jew, Dawidowicz spent time in Lithuania and Poland before war broke out and helped with efforts on behalf of refugees later on.

Terrence Des Pres, *The Survivor*. New York: Oxford University Press, 1976. Reflections on how people survived the death camps; includes frequent excerpts from first-person narratives.

Deborah Dwork and Robert Jan van Pelt, *Auschwitz, 1270 to the Present*. New York: W.W. Norton, 1996. A scholarly and informative history of Auschwitz—the town and the concentration camp.

Harold Flender, *Rescue in Denmark*. New York: Manor Books, 1964. An effective journalistic account of the escape of Danish Jews into Sweden.

Martin Gilbert, *Auschwitz and the Allies.* New York: Holt, Rinehart and Winston, 1981. A history of the Auschwitz concentration camp, with special reference to what the Allied governments knew about it and what they did with that knowledge.

Roger Howard, *Great Escapes and Rescues: An Encyclopedia.* Santa Barbara, CA: ABC-CLIO, 1999. Includes information on several escapes from Nazis as well as other topics.

Wieslaw Kielar, *Anus Mundi.* New York: Times Books, 1972. Kielar spent nearly five years as an inmate in Auschwitz and published his experiences many years afterwards.

Claude Lanzmann, *Shoah: An Oral History of the Holocaust.* New York: Pantheon, 1985. The transcription of a documentary made by Lanzmann on the Holocaust. Lanzmann interviewed survivors, Nazis, and ordinary citizens to make his movie. One of his subjects was Rudolf Vrba.

Walter Laqueur, *The Terrible Secret.* Boston: Little, Brown, 1980. This book investigates how and why the truth about the Holocaust was kept a secret throughout the war.

Hillel Levine, *In Search of Sugihara.* New York: Free Press, 1996. In this book, Levine wonders what drove Sugihara to use his position to help thousands of strangers escape from the Nazis. Part biography, part account of the escapes, and part description of the author's quest for the truth.

Filip Müller, *Eyewitness Auschwitz.* New York: Stein and Day, 1979. Müller was a prisoner in Auschwitz; this is his account of what he experienced in the camps. He was acquainted with Rudolf Vrba and Alfred Wetzler. A moving and effective book.

Mordecai Paldiel, *The Path of the Righteous.* Hoboken, NJ: KTAV, 1993. A comprehensive book about the efforts of gentiles to rescue Jews during World War II. Includes a valuable assortment of quotations from people explaining why they got involved in rescue work.

Richard Rashke, *Escape from Sobibor.* Boston: Houghton Mifflin, 1982. A well-written and well-researched account of the Sobibor uprising.

P.R. Reid, *The Colditz Story.* Philadelphia: Lippincott, 1953. Reid was one of the men who escaped from Colditz in 1942. This breezy, informative book describes life in the prison and tells about the numerous escape attempts undertaken by the prisoners.

Yuri Suhl, ed., *They Fought Back.* New York: Schocken Books, 1967. A collection of first-person accounts of people who fought against Nazi oppression, along with some summaries by the editor.

V. Stanley Vardys, ed., *Lithuania Under the Soviets.* New York: Praeger, 1965. Essays about Lithuanian government, culture, and history between 1940 and 1965.

David S. Wyman, *The Abandonment of the Jews*. New York: Pantheon, 1994. An investigation of the world's unwillingness to help the Jews during Hitler's rule.

Leni Yahil, *The Rescue of Danish Jewry*. Philadelphia: Jewish Publication Society of America, 1969. A well-researched account of the Jewish flight from Denmark. Informative and interesting.

William Zinsser, ed., *Going on Faith*. New York: Marlowe, 1999. About writers and their work as it pertains to spiritual concerns. Includes remarks by Hillel Levine about Chiune Sugihara.

Index

Picture Credits

About the Author

Stephen Currie is the creator of Lucent's Great Escapes series. He has also written many other books for children and young adults, among them *Life in the Trenches* and *Terrorists and Terrorist Groups*, both for Lucent. He lives in New York State with his wife and children. Among his hobbies are kayaking, snowshoeing, and bicycling.